I0605110

TO:
FROM:
DATE:

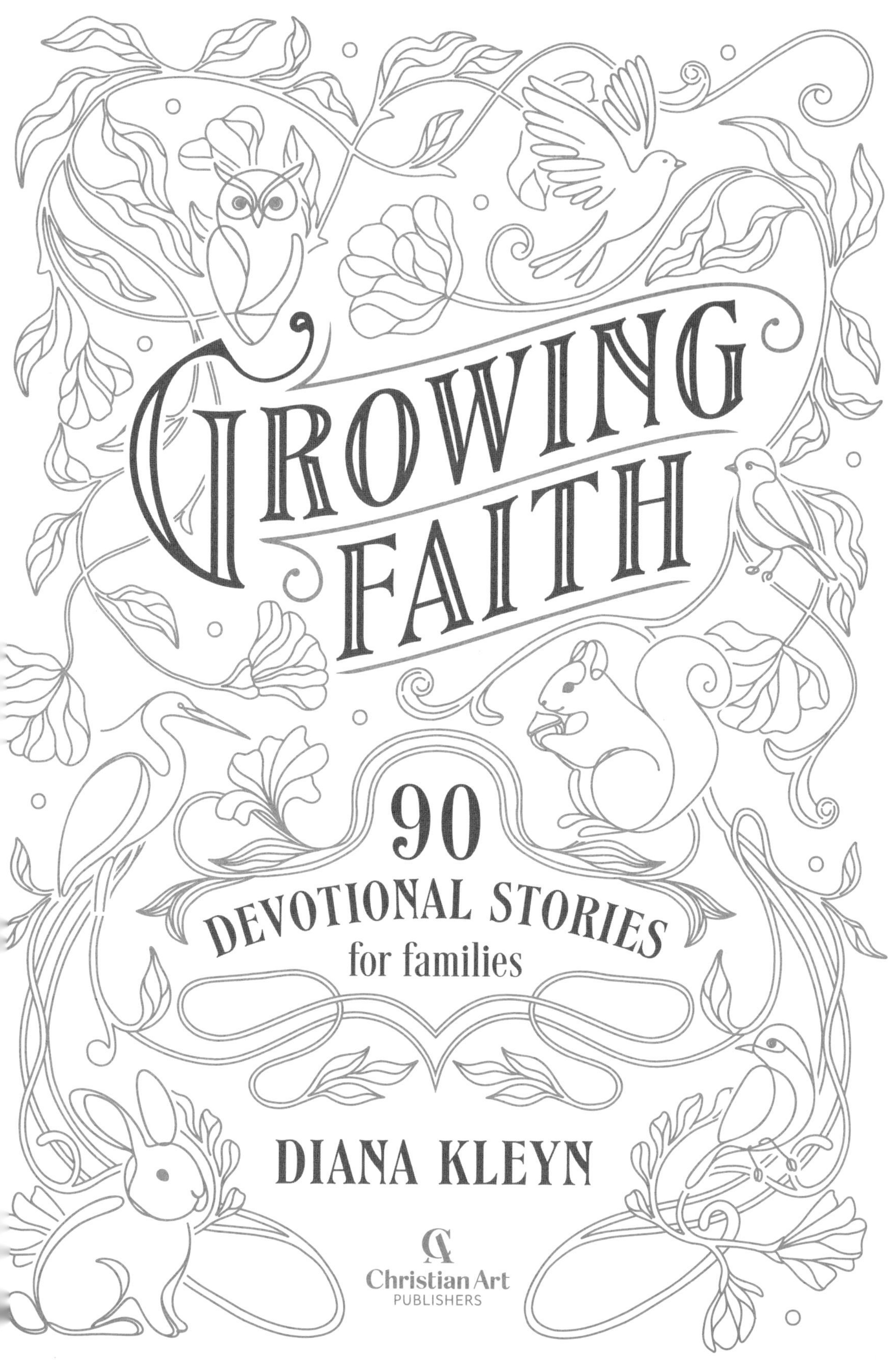

Growing Faith

90 Devotional Stories for families

Diana Kleyn

Christian Art
PUBLISHERS

Visit Christian Art Gifts, Inc., at www.christianartgifts.com.

Growing Faith: 90 Devotional Stories for Families

Adapted from the three-book series titled *The Lord's Garden: Taking Root, Bearing Fruit, and Sowing the Seed* by Diana Kleyn. Copyright © 2019.

Published by Christian Art Gifts, Inc., Bloomingdale, IL, USA under license from Reformation Heritage Books, Grand Rapids, MI.

First edition 2025.

Designed by Christian Art Gifts, Inc.

Cover and interior images used under license from Shutterstock.com.

Scripture quotations are taken from the *King James Version* of the Bible.

Most Christian Art titles may be purchased at bulk discounts by churches, nonprofits, and corporations. For more information, please email SpecialMarkets@cagifts.com.

ISBN 978-1-63952-976-6

Printed in China.

30 29 28 27 26 25
10 9 8 7 6 5 4 3 2 1

Contents

Bearing Fruit

Sowing the Seed

Introduction

The stories in this book have to do with plants taking root, bearing fruit, and then sowing seeds for new plants to grow. The tales are not about actual flowers, leaves, dirt, or fruit, but they are about spiritual plants in the garden of the Lord.

Taking Root

God's people are like plants that grow in His garden. When our hearts are turned away from selfishness and sin to faith in Jesus and devotion to God, we are like a plant that is taken from dry and poisoned ground and tenderly replanted in rich, wet earth. Faith shoots out roots into the new soil so that it can live and take nourishment. The first section of this book includes stories about men and women and boys and girls whose faith takes root in God's good soil and begins to thrive.

Bearing Fruit

As faith grows, it buds into obedience and godliness. In Galatians 5:22–23, Paul describes the fruit of faith as "love, joy, peace, longsuffering, gentleness, goodness, faith, meekness, and temperance." Through His Spirit and the Word, God helps His children to bear good fruit. The second section of the book celebrates stories of how faith bears sweet fruit in peoples' lives.

Sowing the Seed

Good fruit contains good seeds. The final section of this book tells testimonies of God's people sharing the good news of Jesus with others. Not every person is a preacher or teacher or missionary, but every child of God must scatter the seed of His Word as we go about our daily lives. Being a witness for God simply means that we tell others about our Lord Jesus Christ. This good news will not always be received gladly, but we are to keep on telling it—to keep sowing seeds, trusting that God will help some to take root and to bear fruit.

Growing Faith was originally published as three small books. We've selected 30 stories from each of those books to include here. Our hope is that parents and grandparents will read the stories of faith with little ones, or that older kids will explore the stories on their own. As Christians, we need to hear stories of how God plants faith, produces fruit, and then sows gospel seeds through the lives of His people. Take encouragement, dear reader, from these simple reminders of God's goodness in helping His people grow in faith.

Taking Root

—1—

A Little Girl's Sin Found Out

Take with you words, and turn to the Lord: say unto him, Take away all iniquity, and receive us graciously: so will we render the calves of our lips.

—HOSEA 14:2

One Sunday, a minister preached from the Bible "Be sure your sin will find you out" (Numbers 32:23). He said many solemn things about this earnest Bible verse. One of the things this minister said was, "If you do not find out your sin through the work of the Holy Spirit and bring it to Jesus to get it pardoned and washed away through His blood, you may be sure that your sin will find you out and bring you to the judgment seat of God. Then the Judge of heaven and earth will send you away into everlasting punishment."

In church that morning sat a little girl named Rachel. Before leaving for church that morning, Rachel had told her mother a lie. As she sat listening to the minister's words, she thought to herself, "Oh, that terrible lie! I must either bring it to Jesus, or it will find me out at the last day and bring me to punishment!" She became very anxious about her soul's salvation. She could not think of anything else. That night Rachel hardly slept. She tried to pray but did not find any relief. Was God so angry with her that He would not hear her prayer?

The next morning, Rachel made up her mind to go to her minister and talk with him about all she felt and feared. Rachel had to walk several miles in the rain to reach his home. She was warmly received by the pastor and his wife. Then Rachel poured out all her trouble. When she was finished, she said, "Oh, sir, what shall I do with my sin?"

"There is only one thing to do with it, my child," answered the minister, "and that is to lay it on 'the Lamb of God, which taketh away the sin of the world'" (John 1:29). Then the minister knelt down with the little girl and asked the blessed Savior to forgive her sin, and comfort her wounded heart, and give her the help of His grace and Holy Spirit to keep her from sinning in this way anymore.

Rachel went home feeling like a weight had been lifted from her heart. She thought about the passage the minister had repeated to her several times before she left: "I acknowledge my sin unto thee, and mine iniquity have I not hid. I said, I will confess my transgressions unto the LORD; and thou forgavest the iniquity of my sin" (Psalm 32:5). A love for the Lord Jesus began to bloom in her young heart.

QUESTIONS

- Why couldn't Rachel sleep?
- What was the minister's advice?
- Why did Rachel feel happy?

THINK

- Do you think Rachel asked her mother for forgiveness? Why or why not?
- Does God only forgive the sins we confess? Explain.
- What are some ways of being dishonest without actually telling a lie?

PRAYER

Fill me with love for the truth.
Help me to hate lying and flee from it.

—2—

The Pickpocket's Story

Let him that stole steal no more: but rather let him labour, working with his hands the thing which is good, that he may have to give to him that needeth.

—EPHESIANS 4:28

Once at a meeting of the Bible Society in London, a man spoke to the audience. "Gentlemen," he began, "I am happy there is an excellent society such as this, which tries to raise money for Bibles. I thank God for the wonderful work you are doing. Listen for a moment to my story, and you will see that I have a good reason to thank God for the Bible.

"Several years ago," continued the man, "I belonged to a gang of pickpockets. One day, two of my friends and I were passing a church that was full of people. It was the anniversary of the Bible Society. Seeing so many people there, we thought it would be a good chance for us to get a lot of money.

"The church was so crowded that my friends and I got separated from each other. I managed to get into the center aisle right near the front. The Ten Commandments, in large golden letters, were painted on the wall behind the pulpit. The first words that caught my eye were 'Thou shalt not steal.' I stood rooted to the spot. I felt as if God Himself were speaking to me. My conscience troubled me so much that I began to weep right then and there.

"Meanwhile, my friends were trying to get my attention. It was time to get to work! But I forgot all about them. I got out of the church as fast as I could and moved to a part of the city where nobody knew me. I got a Bible, and for the first time in my life I began to read it. It showed me what a great sinner I was; but it also showed me what a great Savior Jesus is. I prayed to Jesus with all my heart. He heard my prayer, and now my sins are forgiven and my soul is safe in Jesus.

"I am going to America, but before I go, I want to give a gift to the Bible Society. May God bless you in the great and wonderful work you are doing."

QUESTIONS

- Why did the man go into the church?
- What was he planning to do?
- What kind of friends did he have?
- Why did the man begin to weep?

THINK

- Why did the man want to give a gift to the Bible Society?
- Why is it important to distribute Bibles?
- In what ways can we steal without actually taking an object from someone else?

PRAYER

Give me a heart that is unselfish.
Help me to hate stealing and to love giving.

—3—

A Change of Heart

He hath shewed thee, O man, what is good; and what doth the Lord require of thee, but to do justly, and to love mercy, and to walk humbly with thy God?

—MICAH 6:8

In 1673, Mr. John Flavel[1] was in London visiting his friend Mr. Boulter, a bookseller. Mr. Boulter told him this true story to encourage him in his work of writing and preaching.

Some time before, a gentleman dressed in flashy clothes entered the shop. He had an air of arrogance and boredom about him which filled the godly bookseller's heart with pity. The stranger asked for books containing plays. Mr. Boulter told the man he did not have any but showed him Mr. Flavel's little book entitled *Keeping the Heart*. He urged the man to read it, telling him it would do him more good than reading plays. The gentleman read the title and thumbed through the pages. Then he exclaimed, "You want me to buy this book? This author is a fanatic!"

Mr. Boulter shook his head. "No, he's not a fanatic. Read the book and you will find him to be a very wise man. You have no right to make a judgment on this book when you haven't even read it," the shopkeeper reasoned.

At last the man gave in and bought the little book, but he told Mr. Boulter he would not read it.

"What are you going to do with it then since you bought it?" asked Mr. Boulter.

"I will tear it up and burn it and send it to the devil," the man replied roughly.

Mr. Boulter responded, "Well then, you should give it back if you are only going to destroy it."

"No, no, I will read it," promised the gentleman.

"If you do not like it after you've read it, you may bring it back and I will give you a full refund," the shopkeeper stated.

1. John Flavel (c. 1628–1691), a Puritan preacher, was born at Bromsgrove and studied at Oxford. His father, Richard Flavel, and his mother both died of the Great Plague in 1665. He became the pastor at Dartmouth but was sent away in the Great Ejection of 1662, continuing, however, to preach there secretly. His preaching was very effective and gladly received because of his simple, earnest messages. In those days of persecution and uncertainty, his cheerful encouragements were a blessing to God's people, and his solemn warnings were used by the Holy Spirit to save many souls.

About a month later, the same gentleman came to the shop. He was no longer rough and rude, but serious and polite. Gone were the flashy clothes; instead he wore a plain but well-tailored blue suit. His demeanor was no longer proud and disinterested, but humble and sincere. "Sir, I most heartily thank you for putting this book into my hands. I bless God who moved you to do it; it has saved my soul. I will always be thankful that God led me into your shop!" Then he bought a hundred more of those books and told Mr. Boulter, "These are for the poor, since they cannot come and buy them."

What a beautiful change of heart the Lord worked in this man's life! The Lord has no end of means of converting lost sinners to Himself. This man was not looking for salvation—he even despised Mr. Flavel's book at first. But God rescued this foolish man from destruction. Maybe you are not rude and disrespectful, but every person needs a new heart. Has your heart been renewed? Have you repented of your sins? Has the Lord Jesus washed away your sins? Look to Jesus for salvation, for He is the only way. Read His Word, and speak to Him in prayer. He has promised that those who come to Him will never be cast out.

QUESTIONS

- Why did the bookseller feel sorry for his customer?
- What book did he recommend? Why?
- What happened to this customer?
- What did the customer buy for the poor? Why?

THINK

- What do we all need? Why?
- How do we get a new heart?
- Do you have a new heart?

PRAYER

Fill my heart with love to Thee. Help me to read and understand books about Thee.

—4—

Martha's Bible

And Jesus answered him, saying, It is written, That man shall not live by bread alone, but by every word of God.

—LUKE 4:4

A young woman named Martha worked at a cotton mill in England many years ago. She was married to an alcoholic who wasted their money on alcohol. All they could afford was a cold, damp basement apartment. Martha worked long hours to earn enough to pay the rent and buy the food. She tried to hide the money, but her husband, David, often found it.

One day, one of the women who worked at the mill asked Martha if she would like to buy a Bible. "You can own a Bible by paying just a little bit each week," the woman told her.

Martha said she would think about it. Martha knew they needed every penny she earned, because her husband, David, did not work. Making a bold decision, Martha decided to go ahead and buy the Bible. After all, she was the one that earned the money, and her mother had always told her it was important to read the Bible. Finally, after many weeks of work, Martha took home her beautiful new Bible. Proudly, she laid it on the table in her home. When Martha's husband came home from spending the evening with his friends, he noticed the new Bible on the table. Martha expected him to scold her for spending money on something that they didn't think was absolutely necessary. David, however, did not become angry. Instead, he seemed almost pleased. He picked it up and opened it.

"Martha, read this story to me," demanded David, who could not read or write. "I've heard people talk about the Bible, but never paid much attention before. I want to know what's in this Book."

So Martha read aloud, and her husband listened. She began at the place where David had opened the Bible—the story of Joseph. They became so interested that they read the whole story before going to bed. The next day was Sunday, and since Martha did not have to work, and they had never gone to church before, they continued reading in the new Bible. They discovered what God says about sin, and what must happen to the sinner if he is not renewed. They began to ask, "Lord, what must we do to be saved?"

Their lives were changed. They went to church. They searched the Scriptures. And the Lord converted them both.

David started a new job. Do you know what it was? He sold Bibles! He visited fairs, races, and marketplaces for the purpose of selling Bibles. He prayed that many so-called "hopeless cases," such as he had been, would be rescued from eternal death through this means. In his lifetime, David sold about 30,000 Bibles and New Testaments. Who can tell the results which followed from the Bible Martha took home on that memorable Saturday night? Thirty thousand Bibles and New Testaments were sold because of David and Martha's conversions. The Lord can bless the simplest means. Ask the Lord to make you able and willing to serve Him.

QUESTIONS

- Why did Martha have to work?
- What did she decide to buy?
- What was her husband's response?
- What did he want Martha to do for him? Why?
- What was the result of their reading?
- What was David's new job?

THINK

- What encouragement does this story offer to those who read the Bible?
- Why is it important to read the Bible every day?
- In what ways (even "small" ways) can you serve the Lord?

PRAYER

Fill me with love for Thee and Thy Word.

—5—

God's Word Satisfies

For he satisfieth the longing soul, and filleth the hungry soul with goodness.

—PSALM 107:9

Situated between the Russian Federation and China is the little country of Mongolia. This country has a long history. Since about the thirteenth century there was a group of people in this country called the Tartars, or Tatars. In the nineteenth century, two Tatar chiefs traveled to St. Petersburg in Russia to learn the Russian language and to study some of the arts and customs of the Europeans. This would be beneficial for them economically, that is, for trading goods and making money. These two chiefs brought with them letters from their tribes, stating that they were trustworthy, honorable men.

A German missionary who was translating a part of the New Testament into the Tatar language was delighted to meet these chiefs and asked them to help him in his work. This immense task kept the three men busy for several months. They asked the missionary many questions about Jesus, the Savior, and the truths He taught.

At last came the day when the translation was finished. The two chiefs sat in silence by the missionary as if they were not willing to leave him.

"Have you any questions to ask, my friends?" inquired the missionary.

"None," was their answer.

"We wish to tell you that we believe the religion of that Book," continued one of the chiefs, pointing to the New Testament which lay on the table. "We have lived in ignorance and been led by blind guides. We have read the books which tell about the religion in our country. But the more we read those books, the less we understood them, and the more empty our hearts became. Your book is very different from anything we ever heard before. The more we read the words of God, the better we understand them. It seems as if Jesus Himself were talking to us. Now we know how to get our sins pardoned, and where to find the help we need in trying to serve Him. That Book satisfies our hearts and makes us feel happy."

What makes you happy? Are you happy? Do you love the Bible? Read the Bible every day, and do not neglect this live-giving Book! Pray for a blessing as you read it.

QUESTIONS

- Why did the Tatar chiefs travel to St. Petersburg, Russia?
- What task was the missionary working at?
- What effect did the Bible have on the chiefs?
- What was the difference between the Bible and the books of the other religions?

THINK

- What is the main message of the Bible?
- Does the Bible have a special place in your heart?
- What effect does the Bible have on your life?

PRAYER

Bless those who translate and bring
Thy Word to people all over the world.

—6—

A Mocking Discussion of the Bible

Wash you, make you clean; put away the evil of your doings from before mine eyes; cease to do evil.

—ISAIAH 1:16

Years ago when America was still a rough, young country, twelve young men set out from England to see this great new land. After a long ocean voyage, the men finally arrived. They worked hard during the summer, but soon winter forced them indoors. As time went on and the nights became long, the men grew bored. They were tired of playing one card game after another. There was nothing else to entertain them in this empty, wild country, so they tried to think of something to amuse themselves. Finally one of the men suggested that they have a mocking discussion of the Bible. Several of the men had tucked Bibles in their suitcases, at the insistence of their mothers, but until now, these Bibles had remained unread. Some of the men protested against the idea of a debate, but others thought it might be fun.

"We'll have to have some of us argue against it and some for it," stated Charlie. "John, you're good at talking. Which side do you pick?"

"But I don't know anything about the Bible!" protested John.

Charlie grinned at him. "Then we'll make you the defendant."

The other men laughed. This might prove to be fun after all! They chose Michael to argue against the Bible. His task was to try and bring out many "contradictions," "faults," and "impossibilities" in God's Word.

At first the men didn't take it very seriously, but as the other ten egged them on each evening, the competition grew more intense. In order to try to win the debate, John began to study his Bible. At first, John studied only to try to win, but the more he studied, the more interested he became by the beauty, majesty, and wisdom of the Book. With each debate, the men could see that John believed the Word more and more fully. He was no longer a mocking, arrogant unbeliever. Joy and peace now reigned in his heart. His speeches about the Bible were heartfelt and persuasive. So great was the effect of his arguments and testimony that other men were brought to a knowledge of the truth as it is in Jesus. The result of this "mocking discussion of the Bible" was that all but one of the men were converted to God.

QUESTIONS

- Why were the young men bored?
- What new idea did they have to occupy their time?
- What did the young men have in their suitcases?
- What happened as they studied for this game?

THINK

- What do you do when you are bored?
- Do you think the mothers were praying for their sons? Why or why not?
- How do the Word and the Holy Spirit work together?
- Is the Bible a treasure to you?
- What are some techniques that can help you study the Bible?

PRAYER

Fill me with awe for Thee and Thy Word.

—7—

Afraid to go Home

Repent ye: for the kingdom of heaven is at hand.

—MATTHEW 3:2

During the mid-1800s, many towns and villages in America experienced the blessings of revival. In one particular congregation, a twelve-year-old boy approached one of the elders after a service. He was greatly distressed and asked the elder for help. The elder asked him what made him feel so distressed.

"My sins, Sir!" exclaimed the boy. "I am a great sinner in God's sight, and I'm on my way to hell! What must I do?" He wrung his hands as tears coursed down his flushed cheeks.

The elder laid a gentle hand on the boy's shoulder. "You must go home and read the Bible, and pray to God to give you a new heart," he advised.

The boy looked up at the elder with alarm in his serious brown eyes. "Sir, I am afraid that if I wait to get home, I may die on the way, and then it will be too late!"

Sympathy and shame filled the elder's heart, and tears sprang to his eyes. He felt reproved by the boy's earnestness. He had a better solution, one he should have given first of all. "Dear child, if you are afraid to go home because you may die in your sins, then you must repent right now and believe in Jesus Christ. When the prison guard asked Paul and Silas, 'What must I do to be saved?' they answered, 'Believe on the Lord Jesus Christ, and thou shalt be saved' (Acts 16:30–31). Let's pray right now. Before you go home, you must submit yourself into His gracious hands."

Together they knelt, both shedding tears. Both prayed, the boy begging God for forgiveness, the elder reminding God of His own promises to repenting sinners. Tears of sorrow turned to tears of joy, and the boy went home rejoicing in his newfound Savior.

Children, are you ever troubled by your sin? Have you ever felt afraid to die, like the boy in this story? Turn, right now, to Jesus and ask Him to cleanse you and forgive all your sin. "If we confess our sins, he is faithful and just to forgive us our sins, and to cleanse us from all unrighteousness" (1 John 1:9).

QUESTIONS

- Why was the boy distressed?
- What was the elder's advice?
- What was the boy's response?
- What did the elder and the boy do then?
- What was the result?

THINK

- Why was the boy's need so great? Do you think he was overreacting?
- What can we learn from this boy?
- Why should we never postpone seeking the Lord?
- How long must we pray for God to hear and answer us?

PRAYER

Show me the necessity of salvation.
Give me Thy salvation.

—8—

Trying to Enter by the Wrong Door

Humble yourselves in the sight of the Lord, and he shall lift you up.

—JAMES 4:10

Robert Murray M'Cheyne of Dundee was a well-known preacher in Scotland. He was known for his holy life and powerful preaching. Once, during one of his sermons, a man who had been anxious about his soul for a long time was blessed with peace from the Holy Spirit. At the close of the service, the man went to Rev. M'Cheyne to tell him the good news. It was clear on the man's face that the Lord had given him peace. The joy of the Lord so filled the man's soul that Rev. M'Cheyne did not even ask if the Lord had forgiven his sins. He simply asked, "How did you get it?"

The man answered, "All the time I have been trying to enter by the saint's door, but while you were preaching, I saw my mistake and entered in at the sinner's door."

Many people make the same mistake. They try to make themselves better for God, at the same time turning their back on the door to Christ. Jesus said, "They that are whole need not a physician; but they that are sick. I came not to call the righteous, but sinners to repentance" (Luke 5:31–32). "The Son of man is come to seek and to save that which was lost" (Luke 19:10).

Children, do not try to make yourself "presentable" or "acceptable" to God. You will never succeed. Come to Him as a sinner, not as a saint. Come as you are; come by faith. Come, trusting in Jesus Christ, and you will receive a free, full, and eternal salvation.

QUESTIONS

- How could Rev. M'Cheyne tell that the Lord had forgiven the man his sins?
- What was the man's mistake?
- What did he mean by the saint's door?
- What did he mean by the sinner's door?

THINK

- How can we come to Jesus as a sinner rather than a saint?
- Can you think of anyone in the Bible who came to Jesus as a sinner? As a saint?
- What happened to them?

PRAYER

Show me that I am a sinner.
Show me also Thy salvation.

—9—

Clean Within

Purge me with hyssop, and I shall be clean: wash me, and I shall be whiter than snow. Create in me a clean heart, O God; and renew a right spirit within me.

—PSALM 51:7, 10

"Mommy," said Katie to her mother one day, "would you tell me how I can be good inside?"

"What do you mean?" asked her mother, surprised by the unusual question.

"I mean that I don't have right feelings in my heart. Daddy tells me I am a good girl, and you call me 'sweetheart.' Everybody thinks I'm good, but I'm not good at all!"

"I'm sorry to hear it," answered Katie's mother.

"So am I," said Katie. "I know my heart is very wicked." Tears filled Katie's eyes. "Yesterday, when I was wearing my favorite dress, I wanted to go for a ride with you and Daddy. He told me that he wanted to spend time with you and that I could go some other time. I went back into the house and waited for you to come back. Aunt Lydia told you I had been very good about it. But she didn't know! I didn't say anything to her, but I went upstairs, and even though I didn't cry, I thought very mean things. I punched my pillow because I was so angry, and I wished the car would break down so you couldn't go for a ride!"

Katie was crying now, and she added in a sob, "Mommy, can't you tell me how I can be good inside?"

Katie's mother hugged her daughter as she explained that Jesus shed His blood to wash away sin. She told Katie that our hearts are like fountains which continually flow with sin. If we want to be clean inside, we need to have the fountain of sin stopped, and that can only happen by God's almighty power. We need a new heart, a heart that is cleansed from sin. God promises to give this: "A new heart also will I give you, and a new spirit will I put within you: and I will take away the stony heart out of your flesh, and I will give you an heart of flesh. And I will put my Spirit within you, and cause you to walk in my statutes, and ye shall keep my judgments, and do them" (Ezekiel 36:26–27). When Jesus determines to save His people, He always begins with the heart. When our hearts are cleansed, then we will obey the Lord and walk in His ways. If you can make a fountain pure, then you may be sure that the streams which flow out from it will be pure also. But we must ask for this gift. God says, "Thus saith the Lord God; I will yet for this be enquired of by the house of Israel, to do it for them" (Ezekiel 36:37). The Lord wants to give you a new heart, but He also wants you to ask Him for it. And He promises that "those that seek me early shall find me" (Proverbs 8:17).

The Holy Spirit was teaching Katie that even though she could keep her lips from saying bad things, she couldn't stop her heart from thinking and feeling bad things. She could be good on the outside, but she was wicked on the inside. After this talk with her mother, the Holy Spirit taught Katie to believe in Jesus Christ, who takes away sin, and makes hearts clean within.

QUESTIONS

- What was Katie's question?
- How was Katie's behavior different than her thoughts?
- What was Katie's mother's answer?
- What was the Holy Spirit teaching Katie?

THINK

- Have you ever felt wicked thoughts even though you obeyed your parents or teachers?
- Why is it not enough to be outwardly obedient?
- Why must we confess our sins to God?

PRAYER

Show me what lives in my heart.
Give me a clean heart.

—10—

The Bird in the Church

I am the door: by me if any man enter in, he shall be saved, and shall go in and out, and find pasture.

—JOHN 10:9

In the center of a large early American town stood a beautiful church. Though America was still a young country, the church was about two hundred years old, one of the first churches built in the New Land. It was surrounded by many trees. High above the tallest buildings rose a tall steeple in which a large clock solemnly chimed the hours. What was even better than its outward beauty, this church had been a true house of worship, where God was worshiped in Spirit and in truth.

One beautiful Sunday morning in late spring, the doors of the church had been left open during the service to allow the fresh breezes in, though the windows remained closed. Just before the service, a bird swooped through the open door and flew up to the vaulted roof. Alarmed by the sight of so many people, and the voices and the music which it heard, it desperately tried to escape.

In one of the pews sat a young lady who noticed the frightened bird. Her gaze followed the fluttering creature from window to window as it vainly sought to escape. It looked for an exit at every window. Then it rose to the ceiling, frantically trying to find a way out of the building. At last, its wings grew weary, and all hope of escape seemed gone. As if unable to keep itself in flight much longer, the little bird flew lower, just above the heads of the congregation. Just then it caught sight of the door, and, in a moment, it was free. The young lady couldn't help smiling as she heard the bird sing a happy song of triumph in the nearby branches of the trees.

When the bird had gone, the thoughts of the young woman turned to herself. Suddenly, she realized she was just like that little bird. "I have been acting like that foolish bird," she thought to herself. "I have been seeking peace in ways and places where there is no peace! I am trying to escape from the punishment of sin by beating against closed windows. I will never be able to pay for my own sin! Christ is the door! Through Him there is escape from sin and from the power of sin. I have acted like that foolish bird far too long. Just as it has escaped through the door of the church, I want to find peace through the Lord Jesus Christ."

From this day on, the Holy Spirit worked in this young lady's heart. She learned that she could never satisfy God by trying to pay for her sin. Her good works were stained with sin. She needed forgiveness and grace from the Lord Jesus Christ. By asking Him for mercy, she was knocking at the Door, and when He forgave her, she was set free.

What about you, children? Are you still beating at the windows, like this little bird, trying to find an escape from sin? Are you even trying to escape at all? Do you try to quiet your conscience by telling yourself that you have plenty of time to repent later, when you are older? Or, do you think you are not really so sinful, that God is kind, and He will overlook your flaws? Those are lies from Satan, and you must never believe them. You do not know how much time you will have; you are far more sinful than you think you are. And though God is kind, He will not and cannot overlook any sin! Flee to the Lord Jesus Christ, the open Door! Tell Him your sins. You may even tell Him that you don't think you are all that wicked, but then ask the Holy Spirit to show you your sins so that you may hurry through the Door and find true peace and freedom in the Lord Jesus Christ. "Then said Jesus unto them again, Verily, verily, I say unto you, I am the door of the sheep" (John 10:7).

QUESTIONS

- How did the bird get into the church?
- How did it try to get out?
- How did it finally succeed?
- What lesson did the young lady learn from this bird?

THINK

- How are we like this bird?
- What lies might Satan be trying to make you believe? Do you believe them?
- If you are not saved, what lies are you believing?
- What are the benefits of fleeing to Christ when we are young?

PRAYER

Lead me to Jesus. Give me grace
to walk beside Thee every day.

"Can I Become a Christian?"

For whosoever shall call upon the name of the Lord shall be saved.

—ROMANS 10:13

In the winter of 1852, a teacher named Mr. John Cooper worked in the school and Sunday School of a town in America. One of his students was a girl named Mary. From her earliest years, Mary's parents had treated her harshly and forced her to work hard. She received no thanks or affection from her family. There was no time to play or make friends. Because Mary's family did not attend church, she did not know the Lord, and she had no one to whom to tell her troubles.

Mary grew into a young lady. She was well behaved and polite, and seemed to have overcome her difficult past. No one knew, however, that in the darkness of the night, she would often cry herself to sleep. She was a very unhappy girl.

One day, Mary stayed after school to finish copying an assignment from the chalkboard. The teacher used this opportunity to speak with Mary about her need of salvation. Mr. Cooper told her that she was a sinner who needed to be washed in the blood of the Lord Jesus. Mary listened politely, but made no answer.

Mary was very good at covering up her feelings. She had learned at a very young age to hide her feelings to avoid punishment. Mr. Cooper only saw her expressionless face; he did not know the thoughts that tumbled through Mary's mind. He did not realize that she was angry. She hated Mr. Cooper. Why did he talk to her like that? Everyone thought she and her family were wicked people because they did not go to church. Religious people like Mr. Cooper thought they were better than Mary. Well, she didn't want to hear what he had to say. She tried to push Mr. Cooper's words out of her memory.

Soon after this, Mary and her family moved away, and Mr. Cooper did not see her for several years. Mary was glad to get away from her teacher. But God, in His providence, arranged that Mary would visit her hometown and meet Mr. Cooper again. Making use of an opportunity to speak with Mary privately, Mr. Cooper once again spoke to her about her soul, urging her to repent and believe. His words were gentle and his tone sincere as he told her about the loving Savior.

This time Mary's response was different. She covered her face in her hands and, with tears in her eyes, lamented, "Can I become a Christian?"

She told Mr. Cooper that no one had ever spoken to her about her need for salvation, and she felt she was too wicked to find forgiveness with God. All these years, since Mr. Cooper had spoken to her, the Holy Spirit had been stirring Mary's conscience. She could never rid herself of his admonitions. Now God brought her face to face with her need. For days, she was in great distress, not daring to reject the gospel, yet fearing the promises were not for her.

Meanwhile, Mr. Cooper and the other Sunday school teachers prayed earnestly for Mary's salvation, wrestling with heartfelt pleadings at the throne of grace. God heard and answered their prayers. Mary began to hope in the power of Jesus' blood, and trusted in Him for her salvation. More and more, she desired to devote herself to the service of the Lord.

Over the years, Mary observed the Christians with whom she came into contact. Although she tried to avoid them, she couldn't help wondering about these people. She gradually realized that their joy was real, not a flimsy, groundless emotion. She became jealous. But then she worried that these joys could never be for her. She hadn't wanted to listen to God. Was it too late?

As Mary struggled and her friends prayed, the Holy Spirit showed her "the Lamb of God, which taketh away the sin of the world" (John 1:29). A new life was given to Mary, and she now understood the deep, thankful joy that all true believers experience.

Mary, who had been hopeless and angry, through the saving work of the Holy Spirit became joyful and happy. Not long after this, she went back to school. Her greatest desire was to use her talents to honor the Lord. She became a teacher, just like her new friend, Mr. Cooper! She loved to tell her students about her favorite teacher, who had taught her the most valuable things of all. He had pointed her to the Lord Jesus Christ, who welcomes sinners, no matter how wicked. Have you been born again? Do you know the joy of true thanksgiving for all that God has done for you, especially salvation? Are you one of God's children? "Thou wilt shew me the path of life: in thy presence is fullness of joy; at thy right hand there are pleasures for evermore" (Psalm 16:11).

QUESTIONS

- Were Mary's parents kind to her? How can you tell?
- Was Mary happy? How do you know?
- Who was Mr. Cooper? What did he tell Mary?
- How was Mary affected the first time he spoke with her? How was she affected the second time?
- While Mary struggled, what were Mr. Cooper and the other Sunday School teachers doing?
- What did the Holy Spirit teach Mary?

THINK

- Mary heard the gospel twice. How many times have you heard the gospel?
- What is your response to the gospel?
- Are you a good example to those around you?
- What is the most important characteristic of a Christian?

PRAYER

Make me a real Christian.

—12—

Little Johnny's First Bible

Thy words were found, and I did eat them; and thy word was unto me the joy and rejoicing of mine heart.

—JEREMIAH 15:16

Johnny lived in Scotland. He did not care much for toy shops and candy stores, but he could never pass a bookshop without wishing he had money to buy something. His little library at home consisted of all kinds of storybooks, but lately, he had begun to long for a Bible of his own. His parents read aloud from the family Bible every day, and they spoke to their children about Jesus and their need to be cleansed by His blood. Johnny thought often of their loving words and asked the Lord to give him a new heart. A love for the Lord and for His Word was born in his young heart.

In those days in Scotland, everyone would go to church carrying a Bible. They would not think of going to church without their Bibles any more than going without their coats. All Johnny's brothers had Bibles to take to church and Sunday school, so why not he? Now that he was five years old, he felt himself old enough to have his own Bible. He must get a Bible—but how, he did not know. It would be no use, he knew, to ask his mother for one. She would say he was too young, and that his brothers were seven before they got theirs. Johnny decided that he would save up his money until he had enough to buy a Bible, and he determined not to go near a bookstore so he wouldn't be tempted to spend his money on other books.

So Johnny saved his money. He asked his parents and neighbors if he could do little chores for them to earn a little money. Often he would empty his piggy bank and pour the money on his bed to carefully count. It seemed the day would never come when he would have enough to buy a Bible. The months passed, and Johnny kept saving. He bought no candy or toys or other books. Finally, on a bright Saturday morning, Johnny told his mother that he wanted to visit the bookshop and that he would be back soon. He did not tell her what he was going to buy; he wanted to surprise her. He skipped happily down the few blocks to the bookstore. He pulled open the heavy door and went inside. After his eyes adjusted to the dim light, he politely asked Mr. Knight, "Sir, do you have any Bibles today?"

"A Bible!" exclaimed Mr. Knight. "Can you read the Bible already?"

"I know some of the words, but not all of them," Johnny admitted.

"What kind of Bible do you wish to buy?"

"A pocket Bible, sir, so I can take it to church with me."

The shopkeeper showed Johnny a very plain black Bible. "How about this one?" he asked.

"No, thank you," answered Johnny. "I'd like a really nice one."

He showed Johnny several little Bibles, and Johnny chose the most expensive one. Mr. Knight gave the little boy a searching look, and said, "Are you able to pay for such an expensive Bible?"

"Yes, sir!" responded Johnny confidently.

"Where did you get the money? Did your mother give it to you?"

"No, sir," answered Johnny. "I..."

"Does she know that you are buying an expensive Bible?"

The little boy's eyes filled with tears. This was not what he expected! "No."

"Did you get the money honestly? Or did you steal it?"

This was too much for Johnny's honest heart. He burst into tears, all the time trying to speak, but he could not. Mr. Knight put Johnny's money on the counter. "I see how it is. Go home and tell your mother to come and see me," he said sternly.

Johnny realized that Mr. Knight thought he had stolen the money! He ran home, threw himself into his mother's arms, crying and unable to speak. His mother was alarmed and begged him to tell her what had happened. She began to unbutton his shirt to find out where he was hurt. He took her hands in his little ones and shook his head. "No, Mommy!" he finally managed to say between sobs.

His mother had become almost frantic, so great were Johnny's tears. "What is it, then? My dear little one, try to tell me what's wrong!"

At last she made out a few words, "Knight—Bible—money—thief."

"You went to Mr. Knight's bookstore, and you wanted to buy a Bible?"

Johnny nodded, still sobbing.

"Did he think you had stolen the money?"

Johnny only cried harder.

Her own eyes filling with sympathetic tears, she took her youngest child on her lap and gently rocked him, stroking his head and back, comforting him until he grew calm. Then he told her the whole story, how hard he had saved his money and how badly he wanted to buy a Bible because it is God's Word. Kissing him tenderly, she put him down on the sofa and told Johnny she would be back in a little while. With firm steps, she made her way to the bookshop.

Mr. Knight saw that she had been crying and stammered, "H-hello, ma'am. What can I do for you?"

"I'm Johnny's mother. He was here a little while ago to purchase a Bible."

The shopkeeper nervously explained what he had done and why he did it. "I didn't think such a little boy would be able to save up so much money on his own. I've never seen anything like it."

"Yes," smiled the woman. "I haven't either. But, you see, Mr. Knight, Johnny loves the Lord. That's why he wants a Bible so badly. He has worked odd jobs around the neighborhood and done without candy and new toys for a year now so that he could buy a copy of God's Word for himself. I am amazed at his determination. You broke his little heart when you accused him of stealing the money," she scolded gently.

"Johnny is not like my other boys," she continued. "He's always loved books. He could read by the age of four. To be able to read the Bible whenever and wherever he wants is his dearest wish."

As she spoke, Mr. Knight's eyes also filled with tears, and he apologized many times. "I had no idea, ma'am," he said. "I'm so sorry. Poor little boy."

"You couldn't have known," answered Johnny's mother kindly.

"You tell Johnny I'm sorry, ma'am," said Mr. Knight. "And could you send your little boy over here? I'd like to talk to him."

Johnny's anxious expression melted into a happy smile when his mother told him what had happened in the bookshop. "May I go right now, Mommy?"

"Of course," she smiled, giving him a hug.

As soon as Mr. Knight saw him, he took Johnny by the hand, patted his head, and asked his forgiveness. There were several customers in the store, and the shopkeeper introduced Johnny to them just like he was the most important client he had and then told them Johnny's story. They all praised him and complimented him on his wise choice, while Mr. Knight took down the Bible and wrapped it carefully. Coming around the counter, he handed Johnny the package, then reached into his pocket and returned the money to a very surprised little boy. "This is for you, my dear boy. Go home now to your mother. Keep the Bible for yourself, and read in it every day, and God will bless you. Keep the money too; I will not take it from you after what I put you through. Come again soon, Johnny! I will not forget you."

Mr. Knight did not forget Johnny; the two became good friends, and Johnny went often to visit Mr. Knight at the bookshop even when he did not need to buy any books. God did indeed bless the reading of His Word to Johnny's heart. From a young age, he served the Lord. When he became a young man, he went to seminary and became a missionary so he could tell people in other countries about the Lord Jesus Christ.

Dear children, how do you spend your money? What do you wish for? Do you have a Bible, and do you read it? Take time to read your Bible, asking the Lord for His blessing, for by this Book you may be made wise unto salvation, through faith in Jesus Christ, and ready and able for every good word and work.

QUESTIONS

- What did Johnny love more than candy and toys?
- What did he want to buy?
- Why was Johnny so upset?
- What did Johnny's mother explain to Mr. Knight?
- How did Mr. Knight treat Johnny when he came back?
- What was the effect of the Bible on Johnny?

THINK

- What is your greatest wish?
- Why is it important to read the Bible every day?
- Why is it necessary to ask for the Holy Spirit's blessing when we read the Bible?

PRAYER

Teach me by Thy Holy Spirit when
I read or listen to Thy Word.

—13—

True Safety

Thy word was unto me the joy and rejoicing of mine heart: for I am called by thy name, O Lord God of hosts.

—JEREMIAH 15:16

Before the Reformation in 1517, most people belonged to the Roman Catholic Church. One of the beliefs of the priests was that ordinary people should not have Bibles. They told the people that the Bible was a very difficult book to understand, and that only very wise people like themselves were able to understand and explain the Word of God.

Of course, we know that this is not true. Certainly, some parts of the Bible are harder to understand than others, but the Holy Spirit is willing to teach anyone who comes to Him in faith. We believe what the Bible itself says, "Out of the mouth of babes and sucklings hast thou ordained strength" (Psalm 8:2). The Lord Jesus Himself called little children to Himself, welcoming them. "Suffer the little children to come unto me, and forbid them not: for of such is the kingdom of God" (Mark 10:14). This is an encouragement for you, children, to seek the Lord while you are young!

During this time, when Bibles were so rare, God chose, in His sovereign good pleasure, to give a man and his wife a Bible. One day this man came home from work and said to his wife, "I have something. You must tell no one, or we will be thrown into prison."

His wife was alarmed and asked what he had brought home. When the man took the Bible from under his shirt, the woman looked frightened. "You must get rid of it as quickly as you can! We may not own a Bible! It is not allowed!"

The man put the Bible behind the dresser. But he could not stop thinking about it. He began to read it. After several evenings of reading the Bible aloud, the man exclaimed, "Wife, if this book is true, we are wrong!"

He went on reading the Bible. He had no idea that all these things were in this forbidden Book! It showed him what a great sinner he was, and he became frightened. "Wife," he exclaimed, "if this book is true, we are lost!"

Still he continued to read the Bible. He began to love this Book. He learned to know and love the Lord Jesus. He found out that what the priests taught was not the way of salvation. Jesus Christ is the only Way of Life! "Wife," he cried, "if this book is true, we are safe!"

Together they rejoiced in the mercy and salvation that only God can give. That was a blessed discovery to make! Those who put their trust in Jesus will never be disappointed.

QUESTIONS

- What encouragement does God give to children to seek Him?
- Why was the man's wife frightened?
- Why were Bibles not allowed?
- Can you recall the three things the man exclaimed as he read the Bible?

THINK

- Do you believe the Bible is true—all of it?
- Has the Holy Spirit shown you things in the Bible that make you sad?
- Has He shown you things in the Bible that make you glad?
- Are you safe?

PRAYER

Give me safety in Jesus.

—14—

A Sermon in the Woods

The wind bloweth where it listeth, and thou hearest the sound thereof, but canst not tell whence it cometh, and whither it goeth: so is every one that is born of the Spirit.

—JOHN 3:8

In a certain part of America, in a little town surrounded by woods, a minister of Jesus Christ was preaching the gospel to a group of villagers. It was in the early days of American history, when towns consisted of only a few log cabins, with fields painstakingly cut away from the surrounding forest. It was a rare privilege to have a visitor, much more so a preacher! The villagers gladly put aside their work and gathered to hear him.

Unnoticed by the group, a stranger on horseback, passing through the forest, heard the sound of the minister's voice. He stopped his horse, and then quietly urged his horse forward. Not wanting to be seen, the stranger kept himself hidden in the shadows of the trees, but ventured close enough to hear what the preacher was saying.

When the minister finished his sermon, the stranger just as quietly turned his horse around and continued his journey without being noticed by the preacher and his audience. At the time, the message didn't seem all that special to the stranger, but he couldn't help thinking about what the minister had said. He had to admit that what he had just heard was true. As he rode along and pondered the message of the gospel, the Spirit of God began to work in his heart. Like waves of the ocean, his sins seemed to wash over him, till he thought he would die of shame and guilt. He got off his horse and fell to the ground, pleading and crying for mercy. He felt he could not continue to live without God's mercy. Like Jacob, he cried, "I will not let thee go, except thou bless me" (Genesis 32:26). How long he lay there, he did not know, but when he got up, he knew the Lord had answered his cries. He knew a wonderful change had taken place in his heart. No longer overwhelmed with sin and guilt, his soul was flooded with love, peace, and sweet communion with God. He was a new creature in Christ Jesus.

He found his horse, who had wandered off looking for grasses and water, and continued his journey, rejoicing in the goodness of God. Toward evening, he arrived at the next town. It was well known for its wickedness, but the traveler needed a place to spend the night. He did not join the townspeople in their drinking and sinful talk, but boldly told them what great things the Lord had done for his soul. The people were astonished; they had never heard such things before. They didn't know what to make of it and wondered aloud whether he was insane. They talked about locking him in the town jail. Hearing what they said, the traveler explained, with a beaming face, "Actually, I haven't been in my right mind until a few hours ago. Now I am set free, and I am very happy. Don't worry about me; I'm not insane!"

The stranger tried his best to relate to them what the traveling preacher had said in his sermon. He told them to flee from the wrath to come. The Spirit of God accompanied his earnest words, and many took the stranger's words to heart. They asked the traveler to stay a while and tell them more of the things of God. His stay was greatly blessed: a revival began that day in the formerly wicked town, and many lost sinners were brought to salvation in Jesus Christ.

QUESTIONS

- What did the stranger on horseback hear?
- What happened as the man thought about the sermon?
- What was his response?
- How did God answer his prayers?
- What happened when the man stopped for the night?

THINK

- Have your sins ever bothered you? What did you do about it?
- Do you know that your sins are forgiven?
- Have you ever spoken to others about Jesus?
- What are some things that keep you from speaking with others about Jesus?

PRAYER

Teach me Thy ways, O Lord.

—15—

Debra's Plan

For the wages of sin is death; but the gift of God is eternal life through Jesus Christ our Lord.
—ROMANS 6:23

A little girl named Debra loved to play in the attic of her home. Debra's father stored extra lumber there so it would stay dry, and her mother stored canned fruits and vegetables for the winter. The rafters were hung with herbs and flowers to dry for later use. In the summer, the winter clothes and blankets were kept there. It was a wonderful place to play. One day, Debra noticed that her mother had canned some spiced apples—her favorite! There were several jars. Would Mommy notice if Debra opened just one jar? Her conscience told her that whether or not Mommy noticed, God certainly would, and that made her feel uncomfortable. Every time she went into the attic, however, those jars of spiced apples made her mouth water. Finally, she decided to open a can, just for one slice of apple. With a nail, she popped open the lid—did anyone hear it? She pulled out one of the beautiful pink rings and put it in her mouth. But somehow, it didn't taste nearly as good as it did last Christmas.

In the attic, hanging above the chests filled with blankets, was an old oil painting. The artist had skillfully painted a man's face, and it seemed that the eyes followed Debra's every move. She used to like the old man's picture, but now she wanted to get away from it. They seemed to scold her, "Oh, I see you, Debra! I saw what you did, and God saw it, too! He says, 'Be sure your sin will find you out'" (Numbers 32:23).

After several days, Debra became so annoyed, that she decided to put an end to the "sermon" these two great, staring eyes preached to her. She brought into the attic a small pair of sharp, pointed scissors, climbed onto the trunks filled with blankets, and cut out the eyes in the painting. "There, now the old man can't scold me anymore!" she thought. But when she looked back at the painting, she saw two dark holes where the eyes had been, and that reminded her of the staring eyes and the sermon they seemed to preach to her. Debra was very unhappy.

The following day, Mom came down from the attic looking very serious. "Debra," she called. "I need to talk to you!"

"Yes, Mommy!" Debra answered guiltily. She suspected her mother had seen the damaged painting.

"I was in the attic just now, and I noticed that the painting had holes in it."

Mommy looks so sad, Debra thought. Tears filled her eyes, and the whole story came out. "I'm so sorry, Mommy," she sobbed. "I wish I never did it!"

"I'm glad to hear you are sorry, but do you see how one sin leads to another?" probed her mother gently. "It started by coveting the spiced apple rings. Then you stole, and because of that you ruined a beautiful painting trying to quiet your conscience. Sin ruins everything—I'm sure those apple rings didn't taste very good, did they?"

"No," admitted Debra. "But worst of all, I just felt so bad inside, in my heart. I don't like that feeling."

"You've apologized to me, dear, and I forgive you, but now you have to ask God for forgiveness," her mother said, handing her a tissue. Then she added seriously, "There's something I want you to remember, Debra. I have forgiven you, and God will forgive you when you confess your sin, but remember this: sin can be forgiven, but the effects remain. What I mean is, all is forgiven, but the painting remains damaged. Sin always leaves behind a painful reminder. Sin is destructive and unpleasant. But remember this, too, my dear daughter: 'The blood of Jesus Christ his Son cleanseth us from all sin. If we confess our sins, he is faithful and just to forgive us our sins, and to cleanse us from all unrighteousness'" (1 John 1:7, 9).

Debra never forgot the lessons she learned that day. In His goodness, the Holy Spirit showed Debra the pain and bitterness of sin, but also the joy of forgiveness. Do you also know this pain and this joy?

QUESTIONS

- Where did Debra like to play?
- What sin did Debra commit?
- What did Debra do to the painting? Why?
- What could an apology not undo?
- What did Debra learn from this?

THINK

- Have you ever felt your conscience bothering you? What made it better?
- Why is it good when our conscience bothers us?
- Do you hate sin? Has it brought you to Jesus?
- Why do we need a Savior?

PRAYER

Make me truly sorry for my sin.
Forgive all my sin.

The Conversion of a "Good Girl"

Not by works of righteousness which we have done, but according to his mercy he saved us, by the washing of regeneration, and renewing of the Holy Ghost.

—TITUS 3:5

Miranda was an eighteen-year-old girl, known for her beauty and her sweet character. She had a kind word for everyone and regularly visited the poor and the sick, always bringing a thoughtful gift with her. Everyone loved her, but she was not pleased with herself.

One evening, at a prayer meeting, her pastor noticed that she seemed troubled. As the meeting progressed, she wept. At the close of the evening, the pastor invited anyone who would like to speak with him to remain behind. Miranda was one of those who stayed.

"Why did you remain behind, Miranda?" asked the minister.

Sobbing, Miranda answered, "My sins!"

Testing her, the minister asked, "But what have you done which makes you weep? You are such a good girl."

At this, she cried out, "No! I hate God, and I know it! I hate Christians, and I know it! I hate my own being! I wish I had never been born!"

The pastor reminded her that there is forgiveness to be found in Jesus Christ, and that her heart could be renewed by the blood of this Savior. He prayed with her, but Miranda could find no comfort. She felt the weight of her sins. Everyone might think she was a "good girl," but she knew the enmity that lived in her heart. She knew that her sins displeased God, and that made her miserable. She had tried to please God by being "good." She had done her best to be kind to others. But the feeling of guilt deep in her heart would not go away. Now she understood that she could not please God by doing good things. She needed her heart to be cleansed.

On her way out of church, she passed through the library. On a ledge lay a little book called *Village Hymns*. In her desperation to find some comfort, she opened it and eagerly began to read the first hymn she saw. This is what she read:

There is a fountain filled with blood,
Drawn from Immanuel's veins;
And sinners plunged beneath that flood
Lose all their guilty stains.

The dying thief rejoiced to see
That fountain in his day;
And there may I, though vile as he,
Wash all my sins away.

Hope flooded her soul. "This is the answer!" she thought. "This is how I can please God! This is the Savior I need!"

Right there in the library, by the grace of the Holy Spirit, Miranda confessed her sin and found forgiveness with the Lord Jesus Christ. When she got up from her knees, her burden was gone. Her enmity to God was gone. Now she was truly a "good girl," not because of her deeds, but because of Christ's sacrifice.

With tears of thankfulness in her eyes, she read the rest of William Cowper's beautiful hymn.

Dear dying Lamb, Thy precious blood
Shall never lose its power
Till all the ransomed Church of God
Be saved, to sin no more.

E'er since by faith I saw the stream
Thy flowing wounds supply,
Redeeming love has been my theme,
And shall be till I die.

When this poor lisping, stammering tongue
Lies silent in the grave,
Then in a nobler, sweeter song,
I'll sing Thy power to save.

QUESTIONS

- Why was Miranda unhappy?
- How had Miranda tried to find favor with God? Why was she unsuccessful?
- How did God show her what she needed?
- What was the result?

THINK

- Why can we never find acceptance with God just by being good?
- Is it wrong to try to be good? Why or why not?
- Do you think people could tell a difference in Miranda? Why or why not?
- Are you good? Why or why not?

PRAYER

Show me why I need to be saved.

—17—

A Sunday School Student

And that from a child thou hast known the holy scriptures, which are able to make thee wise unto salvation through faith which is in Christ Jesus.

—2 TIMOTHY 3:15

One bright spring morning, a woman entered the poor, dirty home of the family of a little girl named Hannah. Hannah was seven years old and attended Sunday school. She was alone and was reading so intently that she did not hear the lady's knock, or even hear her open the door. When she called "Hello!" the little girl finally looked up in surprise.

"Oh, good morning, Miss Barton," exclaimed Hannah. "I didn't hear you knock!"

"Good morning, Hannah. Where is your mother?"

"She went to work and won't be home till supper time."

"Where's Eddie?" asked Miss Barton.

"Mommy took him with her," answered Hannah.

"So there is no one here with you?"

"No, Miss Barton," replied Hannah. "But I don't mind. It gives me time to read."

"What are you reading?" asked Miss Barton, changing the subject.

"I've been learning my Bible verses for next Sunday. I was just reading about Jesus saying, 'Suffer little children to come unto me' " (Mark 10:14).

"Why did you choose that passage, Hannah?" questioned Miss Barton.

"Because last night when I tried to teach my little brother again to kneel down with me and say his prayers, Daddy told me I was not allowed to teach him. You know how those bad men made my dad forget about God, don't you?"

"Yes, dear," responded Miss Barton kindly. "What did you say to your father?"

"I said, 'Daddy, Jesus Christ says, "Suffer little children, and forbid them not, to come unto me." ' "

"What did your father say then?" Miss Barton was amazed at the wisdom of this child.

"Nothing, but he looked very sad. Then I made Eddie say the Lord's Prayer with me."

Miss Barton smiled. "I'm glad. We must pray for your brother and for your parents as well."

Miss Barton and Hannah visited a while longer. Then Miss Barton asked, "Hannah, are you really okay on your own all day?"

Immediately, with sparkling eyes, Hannah replied, "But Miss Barton, I'm not alone! You know that God is with me!"

What a simple, childlike trust Hannah had!

Hannah continued to attend Sunday school. Miss Barton visited many times, speaking with Hannah's parents as well. The Lord blessed these efforts, along with the many prayers on their behalf. After several months, Hannah's family began to attend church services. The Lord converted Hannah's parents, and Hannah's father was no longer influenced by the men who had called themselves friends. They found far better friends among God's children and discovered the reward of serving the Lord.

QUESTIONS

- Why did Hannah not hear Miss Barton's knock?
- What Scripture passage was Hannah reading? Why?
- What was Hannah teaching her little brother?
- Why was Hannah not afraid?
- What changes happened in the family?

THINK

- How was Miss Barton a blessing to the whole family?
- If you were in Hannah's place, would you be faithful?

PRAYER

Make me a blessing to my family.

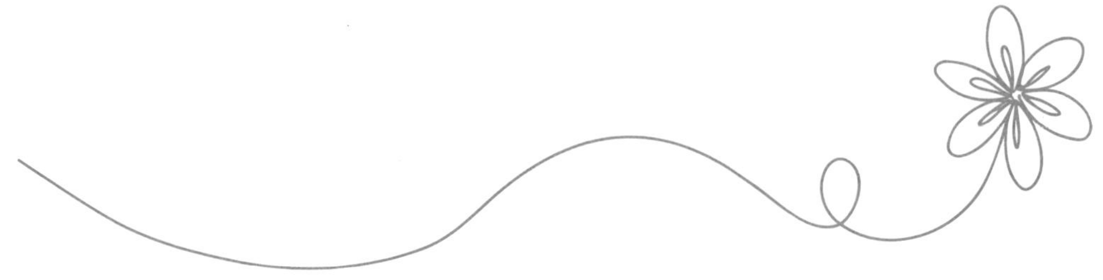

—18—

Torn in Half

Good and upright is the Lord: *therefore will he teach sinners in the way.*

—PSALM 25:8

In France many years ago, a peddler greeted a woman living in a forest cottage and asked her if she would like to buy a New Testament. The woman, named Jeanne, hesitated. Would her husband approve? Wistfully, she eyed the little book and, at last, went inside and got fifty cents to buy it. "I can't refuse this lovely Book, Monsieur," she smiled. "Thank you."

A short while later, her husband, Jacques, who was a charcoal burner in the forest, came home. Timidly, Jeanne showed him her Book. Just as she had feared, Jacques was not pleased. He grumbled that she had wasted so much money on a Book.

"Oh, Jacques, please don't be angry with me. Remember, I brought some money with me when we married. Fifty cents is not all that much money for such a nice Book. Besides, the money is just as much mine as yours, since we're married."

So they argued back and forth. Finally, Jacques snatched the Book from her hands, saying, "Give me the Book!"

Holding the Bible in his hands, he went on, "The money is half yours and half mine. Very well, then the Book is half yours and half mine too!" Angrily, Jacques opened the Book and tore it into two pieces. "Here! One half for you and one half for me!"

Several days later, Jacques was sitting in the forest when he suddenly remembered the torn Book. He felt for his half, which he carried in his pocket. He decided to investigate it right away, so he opened it and began to read. His rough hands had divided the New Testament at the 15th chapter of Luke's Gospel, and the first words that were on his half of the book were, "and will say unto him, Father, I have sinned against heaven, and before thee, and am no more worthy to be called thy son: make me as one of thy hired servants" (Luke 15:18–19).

These were the first words Jacques read, and spellbound, he read to the end of the story. Then a number of questions came to his mind. What had the poor lost son done? Why had he left home? Where had he been? What made him want to go back home? The questions kept churning through his mind, but he knew the answer was to be found in the first half of the Book, and that was in the hands of his wife. Pride kept him from asking for her half.

Meanwhile, Jeanne went about her daily duties. In her spare time, however, she would read in her half of the New Testament. The more she read, the more interested she became, for the Lord had begun to work in her heart. When she reached the end of her half of the Book, she read about the prodigal son: his waywardness, his journey, his sin, his misery, the wonderful change in his thoughts, and then the words, "How many hired servants of my father's have bread enough and to spare, and I perish with hunger! I will arise and go to my father" (Luke 15:17–18), and there the story stopped.

Oh, the questions that ran through Jeanne's mind! What happened to the son? Did the father welcome him or not? Jeanne hoped that the father had welcomed the boy home again, but was afraid to ask Jacques for the last part of the story.

One day, Jacques came home especially tired and ate his supper in silence. At last, he cried out, "Oh, Jeanne, can you forgive me for tearing your Book? I cannot rest until I know the beginning! Would you be so kind as to bring me your part?"

"Oh, Jacques," replied his wife, "the same story is always in my mind too, but I am missing the ending. Did the father receive that poor wayward son?"

"Yes, he did," answered Jacques, "but what was the sin that separated them? Come, bring your part and we'll read the whole story together."

Jeanne brought her half and sat beside her husband. Together they read the whole story of the prodigal son, and the Spirit of God, who had been working in both their hearts already, revealed to them the meaning of the story. They understood that they were prodigals, too, who needed to return to God.

That was the first of many Bible readings together by the fireside after supper. The blessed Holy Spirit pointed them to Christ as their Lord, their Savior, their Substitute, and helped them to arise and go to their Father, who welcomed them, and saved them for Jesus' sake.

QUESTIONS

- What did Jeanne buy from the peddler?
- Why did she hesitate?
- What did Jacques do to the Book? Why?
- At what parable had the Bible been split in half?
- What part did Jacques read? What did he wonder about?
- What part did Jeanne read? What did she wonder about?
- What happened when they finally read the whole story?

THINK

- Read Psalm 76:10. How does this verse apply to this story?
- Are you like the prodigal son or the son who stayed home? Explain your answer.

PRAYER

Help me never to take Thy Word for granted.
Help me to take it seriously and never disrespect it.

Afraid to Swear Alone

Thou shalt not take the name of the Lord thy God in vain; for the Lord will not hold him guiltless that taketh his name in vain.

—EXODUS 20:7

If people are going to steal or do other wrong things, they usually wish to be alone so that no one will see them. But it is different with those who curse and swear and use God's name in vain. They like to swear in public and have many people hear them. Sometimes children and teenagers like to swear and use bad language so that others will be impressed. They think it proves that they are brave and courageous. And yet it is true that those who swear the worst are often the greatest cowards.

A Christian businessman was greatly shocked one day when a man came into his office swearing and cursing in a terrible way. He looked at the man for a while and then said to him, "My friend, I will give you a pocket full of money if you will go into the village churchyard at midnight tonight and swear those same oaths there that you have just spoken here, when you are all alone with God."

The man was surprised. "Agreed," he said. "That's an easy way to make some money!"

"Come back here tomorrow," said the Christian businessman, "and tell me if you did it, and I will give you the money."

At midnight the man started for the graveyard. It was a very dark and dismal night. As he entered the churchyard, not a sound could be heard. All was as still as death. Around him, he could see the reminders that death is real—the tombstones of former villagers cast shadows in the darkness. The church itself seemed to proclaim that God is not dead, as the man had tried to tell himself. Then the Christian man's words, "when you are all alone with God" rang in his ears. He began to tremble. He felt that God was right there, close by his side. He was terrified! The idea of cursing and swearing when God seemed nearer than ever terrified him. He did not dare to utter a single oath. Instead, he ran home, dashed up the stairs to his bedroom, and fell on his knees by his bed. "God, be merciful to me, a sinner!" he wept. He spent the night wrestling with God, begging for forgiveness of his sins. And God, in His infinite kindness and mercy, forgave also this man.

Never think that your sins are too many for God to wipe away. Do not stay away from the precious Savior, who gladly receives sinners. "If thou, Lord, shouldest mark iniquities, O Lord, who shall stand? But there is forgiveness with thee, that thou mayest be feared" (Psalm 130:3–4).

QUESTIONS

- Why was the Christian businessman shocked?
- What did he challenge the man to do?
- Why was the man unable to carry out the challenge?
- What was the result?

THINK

- Do you ever curse or swear?
- What do you do when others curse or swear?
- Why is it important that a Christian use clean, pure language?

PRAYER

Keep me from speaking in
any way that dishonors Thee.

—20—

The Sailor's Bible

Thy word is a lamp unto my feet, and a light unto my path.

—PSALM 119:105

After returning from a voyage, a sailor visited a shop to buy his wife a gift. He noticed a Bible lying on the counter and inquired, "What is the title of that book?"

The shopkeeper answered, "That is a Bible, sir. Would you like to buy it?"

"A Bible?" echoed the sailor. "Yes, I would very much like to buy it."

The shopkeeper, knowing that few sailors were educated, asked politely, "If you don't mind my asking, can you read, sir?"

"No, I can't," frowned the sailor, "but it would look very respectable to have a Bible in our house."

The shopkeeper was surprised, but was glad to make a sale. The sailor carried the Bible home, thinking his wife would be delighted with the gift. She couldn't read either, but he was convinced that putting it on the little table near her chair would make quite an impression on anyone who came to visit.

When he presented the Bible to his wife, however, she was not at all pleased. Rather, she was angry.

"Why did you waste your money on something that neither of us can use? You could have bought something useful!" So, instead of being a source of pride, the Bible was a source of strife between them. It did not rest on the little table by the woman's chair, but in a drawer in the spare room.

Soon after this, two men from a Bible Society knocked on the door. They asked the sailor's wife if she would like to support the Bible Society or buy a Bible. The very mention of the word "Bible" reminded her of her husband's gift to her, and she angrily informed the men that she already had a Bible which neither she nor her husband could read. The men talked to her about the value of the Bible and how much wisdom was to be found in its pages. Thinking the men were talking only of its material value, the woman became interested. Perhaps her husband hadn't been so foolish after all, she thought. The men urged her to attend a local school which offered classes teaching adults to read. She promised the men she would do so.

It was not long before the sailor's wife was reading without much difficulty. Proudly, she read aloud a chapter every evening to her husband. The sailor was so impressed that he decided he would also attend the reading classes. He, too, quickly learned to read.

As you know, simply reading the Bible is not enough for salvation. But the Holy Spirit blessed these evening readings to the hearts of both the sailor and his wife. They began to understand that the men from the Bible Society were not talking about the outward value of the Bible, but its eternal value. The Holy Spirit began to teach them the truths found in the pages of God's Word.

The sailor and his wife began to go to church, and there they learned more about themselves and about God. Most importantly, they learned about the Lord Jesus Christ who calls sinners to Himself. How ashamed they were to think that they had only wanted a Bible to look respectable! How glad they were that they had been taught by the Holy Spirit what the Bible says!

Do you know what the Bible says? Do you believe that the Bible speaks the truth? Have you repented of your sin? Do you love to read the Bible? To be able to read the Bible is a great blessing, but it is a greater blessing to be taught God's Word by the Holy Spirit. "Search the scriptures; for in them ye think ye have eternal life: and they are they which testify of me" (John 5:39).

QUESTIONS

- Why did the sailor buy a Bible?
- Was his wife pleased? Why not?
- What did the men from the Bible Society tell the woman?
- What misunderstanding did she have?
- How did God use this misunderstanding to bless the couple?

THINK

- How many Bibles are in your house?
- What does the Bible mean to you?
- Why must we read the Bible every day?

PRAYER

Help me never to get tired of Thy Word
but to love and treasure it more every day.

—21—

"What If It Had Been You?"

Be ye therefore ready also: for the Son of man cometh at an hour when ye think not.

—LUKE 12:40

When Edward Brown was about ten years old, an event occurred in the village where he lived, which he never forgot. Perhaps it will be something you will never forget either. Among the children of the village was a little girl named Alice, about four years of age. If you would have passed by her house on a bright spring morning, you would have seen her playing in her yard, picking dandelions, talking to her doll, or watching the robins eat their breakfast.

Alice had learned from her earliest days to love the Savior. Young as she was, she knew her heart was sinful and needed to be renewed. She loved to hear the Bible stories and tried her best to learn Bible verses and songs about the Lord. When people came to visit her parents, she would talk to them in her childish way about the Lord Jesus, the friend of children.

Across the far side of the garden ran a beautiful stream of water. It was pleasant to look at as it hurried along, with the garden flowers bending over it. Little Alice sometimes played near the garden, but was never left there alone, as her parents were afraid she might fall into the stream. It was not very deep, hardly waist high, but enough to cover her should she fall down.

One morning, Alice had slipped unnoticed into the garden and, not realizing the danger, began to play along the bank of the stream. Happily, she picked flowers and watched the stream bubble merrily on its way, when suddenly her foot slipped, and she fell. No one heard her cry. There could have been only a short struggle in the fast-moving stream, and then it was over. They found her soon after, lying face down in the water. Gently, they lifted her out of the stream, and smoothed back the wet hair from the precious little face. There was no doubt that one more little lamb had gone home to the Good Shepherd, and they knew that the voice which would no more be heard on earth was already mingling with the joyful voices of the redeemed in heaven.

The sad story of Alice's drowning spread like wildfire though the village. Edward Brown soon heard it, and with a grieving heart he ran home to tell his mother.

"Yes, my son, I have heard all about it," she answered, with trembling voice and tearful eyes. "Dear little Alice has been taken home by her Savior. She loved to sing and speak about Him for her heart was full of Him. There's no question that she is rejoicing with the angels in heaven. But Edward," she added solemnly, turning to look her son full in the face, "what if it had been you?"

That was all Edward's mother said to him that day about little Alice. Edward grew up, got a job, married, and had children, but he never forgot his mother's earnest question all those years before. It went straight to his heart, and the Holy Spirit used that question to awaken him to the reality of death and life after death. From the day his mother asked that solemn question, Edward thought seriously about his soul. Anxious thoughts filled his heart. Was he prepared to meet God? What if it had been he who had died that day? The Holy Spirit led Edward to see the wickedness of his heart, but also to experience the forgiveness found only through the blood of the Lord Jesus Christ. He has often told his children the story of Alice and asks them the same question his mother asked him all those years before, "What if it had been you?"

QUESTIONS

- Who was Alice? What did she love to do?
- What happened to her?
- What question did Edward's mother ask him?
- What effect did that question have?

THINK

- What would happen to you if you were to die today? Why do you think so?

PRAYER

Prepare me to meet Thee.

An Unexpected Change

And let us not be weary in well doing: for in due season we shall reap, if we faint not.
—GALATIANS 6:9

This story was written by a minister who lived in America in the colonial days.

For the first eighteen years of my ministry I pastored a country village, which was surrounded by several family farms. Within a mile and a half of the parsonage lived Mr. and Mrs. Blythe and their children. Mr. Blythe grew up during a time when few schools were found in the county, and he could neither read nor write. He had always been a good husband and father, a hard worker, providing a comfortable home for his family. Although the Blythes regularly attended church, they did not seem to understand the need for salvation. I felt great concern for this family and often visited them, trying to explain the simplest truths of Scripture to them. I prayed that the Holy Spirit would open their eyes to see their need of a Savior. All my prayers and efforts, however, seemed to be in vain. Both Mr. and Mrs. Blythe seemed content with their lives and felt no need to seek the Lord. I visited them less and less often, so that I could give my time to others who were more ready to receive the truth.

One evening, when I was slowly making my way home on horseback through the pine forest which surrounded the Blythe farm, I wondered if I should visit the Blythes again. I wanted to try once more to awaken them from their sleep of death. They were at home when I arrived and welcomed me into their home. I soon stated the purpose of my visit, warning them of the danger of putting off repentance and salvation. To my surprise, however, instead of showing the usual lack of interest in what I was saying, I was delighted to see that Mr. and Mrs. Blythe showed great concern for their souls. They were filled with sorrow for ignoring God's warnings for so many years. They asked, "What must we do to be saved?"

My heart overflowed with joy and gratitude to God for His mercy. In my blindness, I had thought these people were hardened beyond hope. With humble thanksgiving in my heart, I read and explained the Scriptures and prayed with them.

Just before I left, I asked them, “Is there a particular incident or event that caused you to begin feeling concern for your souls? What was the turning point?”

They told me that their children had attended a Sunday school in town for two years. On Sunday afternoons, the older children would take turns reading the Bible and Christian children’s books aloud to the younger children. This simple means of grace had reached their hearts. They had been led by the Holy Spirit to see that they were sinners and lost without the Lord Jesus Christ. Now they wanted to know if and how they could find grace and mercy with God. Of course, I gladly explained once again the wonderful story of Christ’s sacrifice for sinners.

After this, I visited them often and rejoiced to see them growing in grace with their children. They became members of the church and were a blessing to many, both in the church and in their community.

Never assume that the time of grace is past for anyone. Also, never let Satan deceive you into thinking that you have sinned too much or too long for the Lord to save you. The Lord can reach the hardest hearts. He delights in mercy (Micah 7:18). “For thy mercy is great above the heavens: and thy truth reacheth unto the clouds” (Psalm 108:4).

QUESTIONS

- What did Mr. and Mrs. Blythe not understand?
- How was this one visit from the minister different from the previous ones?
- What began to soften the Blythes’ hearts?
- What lesson did the minister learn?

THINK

- Why should we never give up hope in God?
- What must we do to be saved?
- Are you saved? Whether yes or no, what are you doing about it?

PRAYER

Make Thy salvation real to me.

—23—

The Gardener's Glad Moment

Therefore watch, and remember, that by the space of three years I ceased not to warn every one night and day with tears.

—ACTS 20:31

A teenage boy named Edward worked as an apprentice to a gardener in Edinburgh at a beautiful home with a lovely garden. Other young people worked there too, and before long, Edward had made new friends. The problem, however, was that these new friends introduced Edward to a lifestyle that was not pleasing to God. Instead of listening to his conscience, Edward went along with his new friends to places he had no business visiting. He wrote fewer and fewer letters to his parents, stopped going to church, and never read his Bible.

One Sunday afternoon, sitting in a bar, Edward thought, *If this doesn't stop, I'll be lost. This is not how I used to spend my Sundays at home.* He thought sadly about his loving family and the godly training his parents had carefully given him. *If I were to die now*, he thought, *I would wake up in hell.*

The thought frightened him, and he decided he needed to change his ways. He left his job in Edinburgh, determined to reform. He moved to Glasgow, where he got a new job. Although he tried to be "good," he found no peace. He became a well-behaved young man, respected for his good morals, but he felt no joy in his heart, no peace that only the Holy Spirit can work. Things went on this way for several years. At first, Edward was quite satisfied with himself, but then he began to wonder if he could stand the test of God's judgment. He began to feel uncertain of his "goodness."

Around this time, he moved on to yet another job in Scotland. He was introduced to his new fellow worker and teacher in the garden and soon found out the man was a Christian. Though Edward had a feeling things were not right in his own heart, he foolishly thought he did not need godly advice and correction. Solomon has many things to say about foolishness in the book of Proverbs. "Wisdom is too high for a fool" (24:7). "The foolishness of man perverteth his way: and his heart fretteth against the LORD" (19:3). "The way of a fool is right in his own eyes" (12:15).

"The fear of the LORD is the beginning of knowledge: but fools despise wisdom and instruction" (1:7).

"Well," Edward thought to himself, "that old man will not influence me!"

However, God had plans of mercy toward Edward. The Holy Spirit was softening the young man's heart. Already on the first day of Edward's new job, the old gardener spoke to the young man about eternal matters and pointed out the necessity of the new birth. The old man had a gift for weaving spiritual lessons into their daily gardening tasks; he pointed out the marvels of God's handiwork and related them to matters of the heart. Instead of feeling angry with the old gardener, Edward felt drawn to him. The man was so kind and meek that Edward listened like a child. He began to realize that something was missing in his life. His sins began to trouble him, and he felt empty and restless. He felt he would give everything he had to have the burden of sin removed. Day after day, as he dug in the damp earth, planting seeds and pulling weeds, the thought haunted him: "Not saved, not saved! One day I will return to the dust and where will my soul be?"

After a week of great anxiety, Edward was sitting by the fireplace one Sunday evening, reading his Bible. Edward read page after page as the Lord spoke to his soul. Text after text sank deep into his aching heart. "Come now, and let us reason together, saith the LORD: though your sins be as scarlet, they shall be as white as snow; though they be red like crimson, they shall be as wool" (Isaiah 1:18). He read more and more passages. At length Edward climbed the stairs to his bedroom and closed the door. Pouring out his heart before the Lord, he confessed his sin and his need for the cleansing blood of the Lord Jesus. A peace he had never known filled his heart. "Behold, God is my salvation; I will trust, and not be afraid: for the LORD JEHOVAH is my strength and my song; he also is become my salvation. Therefore with joy shall ye draw water out of the wells of salvation" (Isaiah 12:2–3). The Lord never disappoints those who come to Him, confessing their sin. Those who put their trust in Christ alone will never regret it.

QUESTIONS

- What effect did Edward's friends have on him?
- Why did he leave Edinburgh to move to Glasgow?
- Why was Edward still not happy?
- Why did he not like the old gardener at his new job? How did that change?
- What did Edward finally do?
- What was the result?

THINK

- Are you like Edward in Edinburgh, in Glasgow, or at the end of the story?
- What effect do your friends have on you?
- What effect do you have on your friends?

PRAYER

Help me to choose friends who will be a blessing to me.
Help me to be a blessing to my friends.

—24—

Prayers for Salvation

So then every one of us shall give account of himself to God.

—ROMANS 14:12

There was once a girl, whom we will name Deborah, who had godly parents. They loved their daughter very much, and desired her salvation. They prayed constantly for her. Though they made every effort to make sure she was well clothed, fed, and educated, their main concern was that she be saved. Deborah knew this, and she came to a very wrong conclusion. She decided that because her parents loved her so much and prayed every day for her salvation, she didn't need to pray for herself. She thought, "God loves my father and mother very much, and certainly He will hear their prayers. I don't have to pray for myself, because their prayers are good enough. I will never be lost, since so many prayers are offered to God on my behalf by such godly parents." It was not that she did not want to be saved—she did, or so she thought. But she forgot that no one can earn salvation for another person. She felt quite safe simply because her parents prayed for her. The Holy Spirit often touched her conscience, but she reasoned that she didn't have to beg for mercy or wrestle in prayer, because her parents did it for her.

God, in His loving mercy and great patience, saw the danger Deborah was in. He did something that did not seem loving: he took away her beloved mother. From that moment, Deborah later said, she felt as though half her dependence was gone, but still, she leaned upon her father's prayers. She believed her father could be her intercessor. Then, again, God did something for Deborah that did not seem loving: her father became sick, and after a time of illness, he died. At last, Deborah felt that every prop was removed. She had no one left to pray for her! She had no one to depend on! Her father was not yet buried. He lay in the coffin. No longer could he pray for his daughter. Deborah was filled with panic. Who would pray for her? She was alone, unprotected! Now, finally, she saw her danger. Falling down on her knees, she cried out to God, "Lord, save me, or I perish!" She told the Lord that she did not dare to get up from her knees until He saved her. How long she stayed on her knees she did not know, but the Lord graciously heard Deborah's prayers.

Was it Deborah's prayer that saved her? No. May we not pray for one another? Yes, we must! But God had to teach Deborah that her parents could not save her. It is God who saves; it is Jesus Christ who intercedes; it is the Holy Spirit who teaches us to cry out to Him. When the Lord taught Deborah this, she cried out to Him, and then the Lord was pleased to answer her prayers.

Do you pray? Or are you like Deborah, foolishly thinking that your parents' or grandparents' prayers are good enough for you? Do you make the mistake of thinking that God will save you because you have godly ancestors? While it is a blessing to have godly parents and family members who pray for you, you must never build your hopes on this like Deborah did. Go to God in prayer and ask Him to make you one of His dear children.

QUESTIONS

- What incorrect conclusion did Deborah reach?
- What two things did God do that did not seem loving?
- Why did Deborah panic?
- What did she finally learn?

THINK

- Why do we need to pray for ourselves?
- Why do we need to pray for others?

PRAYER

Teach me to pray—for myself and for others.

—25—

The Watchword

Unto you therefore which believe he is precious.

—1 PETER 2:7

In one of the great rock passageways of the fortress of Gibraltar, two British soldiers were assigned as midnight guards at each end of a long tunnel in the fortress. One of them was a happy Christian, rejoicing in the peace which he had found in Jesus. The other was distressed with the burden of his sins. He had, for a long time, felt the need of a Savior, but he had never come to Jesus, and was a stranger to "the peace of God, which passeth all understanding" (Philippians 4:7).

In the silence of the night these soldiers were doing their rounds. One of them was meditating on the atoning blood of Christ, which had brought peace to his soul. The other was groaning under the burden of his sins and longing to be rid of that burden.

Suddenly, an officer came in sight. In passing the first sentinel, the officer paused, and asked for the watchword. The startled soldier, forgetting for the moment what the watchword was and thinking only of the peace that filled his soul and of the source from which it came, exclaimed, "The precious blood of Christ!" (1 Peter 1:19). Then, correcting himself, he gave the real watchword, and the officer passed on, greatly wondering, no doubt, at the soldier's words.

But those words the soldier had spoken rang through the tunnel and reached the ears of the soldier posted at the other end. They entered his heart, and it seemed to him as if an angel from heaven had sent him this message: "The precious blood of Christ!" He knew this was what he needed. In penitence and faith he turned to Jesus. His burden rolled off at the foot of the cross, and his soul found rest.

QUESTIONS

- Where were the two soldiers stationed?
- Describe the two soldiers.
- What did the officer request?
- What answer did he receive? Why?
- How did God use this mistake?

THINK

- Why was this message so powerful?
- What does the blood of Jesus mean to you?

PRAYER

Help me to love and treasure the Lord
Jesus Christ and His sacrifice for sin.

—26—

The Siberian Leper

And if thou draw out thy soul to the hungry, and satisfy the afflicted soul; then shall thy light rise in obscurity, and thy darkness be as the noon day.

—ISAIAH 58:10

Siberia is a very cold region. It is also very large: more than thirty-six hundred miles long, and nearly two thousand miles wide. It is not a very easy place to live, since the ground is mostly covered with snow, and the rivers are frozen over for more than half a year. Few flowers are found in the land, and the trees bear little fruit. Most of the year, it is like a frozen desert.

As they did in Mongolia, the Tatars also lived in Siberia. They would rarely settle in towns, but wandered about from place to place, living in tents. Most of these Tatars followed the false prophet Mohammed or a Buddhist monk named Lama. They also bowed before gods of wood and stone made by their own hands.

Missionaries sent to Siberia attempted to teach the Tatars about the true God of heaven and earth and His only Son, the Lord Jesus Christ. God blessed the work of these missionaries, and some of these people became Christians. One day a missionary approached a group of Tatar tents, when he saw a man lying on the ground, nearly dead. He was a leper. Leprosy is a sad disease: the body is covered with large white sores; slowly, the body wastes away. Almost always, the leper was shunned, since there were no hospitals willing to treat him, and his own family turned from him in disgust. This leper, too, was left to perish alone.

When Jesus lived on earth, He had pity on lepers. Love for Christ leads His people to feel compassion for suffering people too. Now, when the missionary saw this poor leper, he wanted to help him. The man looked up at the missionary as he approached, and a look of joy came over his face. "I know you," he cried.

"How can that be?" asked the missionary, thoroughly surprised. "Have you seen me before?"

"Yes, I have," replied the dying man eagerly. "Didn't you preach in a marketplace once in the big city?"

"I could have, but I don't remember," answered the missionary.

"Don't you remember standing on the steps of a house, preaching to some people?" prodded the man.

"Yes, I think I remember it now," smiled the missionary.

"You told us about Jesus who died to save sinners," said the leper. "You said that men of every nation may come to Him, and that He would receive and save them. Oh, sir, I never heard such wonderful things before. I believed in Him that day. He is my Savior, and soon I will be with Him forever. I am dying. No one will help me now, but I have Jesus. That is enough."

Touched by what he had heard and seen, the missionary went into one of the tents nearby, where he found several Tatars drinking. He asked them, "Why do you not go to your brother? He lies there dying with nobody to help him!"

"Brother!" they sneered, "He is no brother of ours! He is a dog!"

Again, the missionary tried to move these men to feel some pity for their fellow Tatar, but they refused to help. So the missionary went back to the poor leper, to try to comfort him. Not long afterward, the man died. Since there was no one to bury him, the missionary dug a grave and gently placed the diseased body of the poor leper into the ground. There his body will lie till the great judgment day, when the Lord will give him a new body to glorify Him forever.

With tears of joy, the missionary thanked the Lord for allowing him to be with the leper as he died. He marveled how the Lord planned this for the poor Siberian leper. Though the man was rejected by his family and friends, God brought a fellow Christian to his side to comfort him in his last moments and bury him after he died. The missionary went on his way, rejoicing at God's mercy, thanking Him that the poor Siberian leper was now in heaven and would not have to suffer any more disease and neglect. "And God shall wipe away all tears from their eyes; and there shall be no more death, neither sorrow, nor crying, neither shall there be any more pain: for the former things are passed away" (Revelation 21:4).

QUESTIONS

- Where did this story take place? What is Siberia like?
- What was wrong with the man left all alone?
- What did the leper tell the missionary? Where had he seen him?
- Why did no one help the leper?
- How did God provide for this leper?

THINK

- In what way was the missionary like Jesus?
- What kinds of people does our society shun?
- Whom do you avoid? What would Jesus say about that?

PRAYER

Give me a heart that loves God
above all and my neighbor as myself.

—27—

The Mathematician Confounded

Wherefore do ye spend money for that which is not bread? and your labour for that which satisfieth not? hearken diligently unto me, and eat ye that which is good, and let your soul delight itself in fatness.

—ISAIAH 55:2

At one of the first colleges in America, a young man had graduated and was honored for his achievements, especially his knowledge of mathematics. This young man found a good job and settled in a town where a faithful minister of the gospel also labored.

It was not long before the minister met him on one of his evening walks, and after they had talked awhile, the minister understood that the young man was not in any way religious. Rather, the man had dreams of becoming rich and famous, living only for this world.

Praying for wisdom, the pastor spoke up as they were about to part ways. "I have heard that you are noted for your mathematical skill. I have a problem which I would like you to solve."

"What is it?" the young man inquired eagerly.

The minister answered, looking compassionately at the young man, "'What shall it profit a man, if he shall gain the whole world, and lose his own soul?'"

The young man was speechless. He had not expected a question like this! He returned home and tried to shake off the impression of this burning question, but he could not. He tried to drown it by going to parties, by studying harder, and by working late into the night, but the question remained: "What shall it profit a man, if he shall gain the whole world, and lose his own soul?"

Thankfully, the young man did not continue to resist the Spirit's knocking, but by God's grace he yielded and was saved. Later, he became a minister and defended the same gospel which he had once disdained.

QUESTIONS

- What was the young man honored for?
- What did the pastor realize about the young man?
- What question did the minister ask him?
- How did the young man try to drown out the question?
- What was the result?

THINK

- What are some gifts and talents God has given you?
- Could the young man have honored God by being a mathematician? Why or why not?
- How can you honor God with your talents?

PRAYER

Help me to honor Thee with
everything I think, say, and do.

—28—

The Hour Alone with God

All scripture is given by inspiration of God, and is profitable for doctrine, for reproof, for correction, for instruction in righteousness.

—2 TIMOTHY 3:16

A godly father had an ungodly son. The father had raised John in the fear of the Lord, reading the Bible to him often, praying and talking with him, but in spite of his father's faithful teachings, John turned his back on the Lord. He hardened his heart against his father's gentle pleadings, stern warnings, and tearful prayers. He chose friends who led him further into sin and who did not care that they sinned against God.

At last John's father became ill. John came to see his father, for though he did not obey him, he did love him. Before he died, John's father asked him, "My son, would you promise me something? It would ease my suffering and give me some comfort."

Hesitantly, John agreed. "What do you want me to do, Father?"

"Just this, dear son. Will you promise me that, after I die, you will spend an hour alone in your room every day?"

"That's it?" John asked in surprise. "What do you want me to do there? I suppose you want me to pray or read the Bible or something."

"Just an hour alone in your room," repeated his father weakly.

John thought it was a very strange request, but was relieved that he didn't have to promise to do anything religious. "I promise to do that for you, Father. You've been so good to me; that will be easy enough to do for you."

Not long after this, the father died. John kept his promise, determined to keep his word. He knew he had caused his father much grief and wanted to do at least this much for him. An hour alone in his room—what was he going to do during that hour? At first, he spent the time straightening out his room. He found some books his father had given him, but he did not want to read them. He put them back on the shelf. Another time he played cards by himself, but he soon tired of that. Sometimes he fell asleep. Other times his thoughts wandered. He thought about his mother, who had died when he was a young boy. He remembered some of the songs she had taught him. He thought about his father, who had been so faithful in teaching him about the Lord. His conscience stung when he remembered his father's tears. He had treated his father rudely and had said some cruel things. He cringed when he thought that he could never ask him for forgiveness.

Once, he brought his father's Bible with him to his room. He remembered how his father had loved to read it, and when he was too tired to read, he would keep it close beside him. Gently, John stroked the Bible's worn cover, but did not want to read it for himself. There were times when John tried to push away the pangs of conscience. Did he really want to give up his friends and his lifestyle to become one of those religious people like his father had been? True, he wasn't enjoying himself lately like he had before his father's death. He'd been telling his friends that he needed time alone, that he missed his father. His friends didn't understand and told him he should be glad he was rid of "the nagging old man." John resented the way they spoke of his father, and it bothered him that his friends didn't seem to miss him. They called on him less and less often.

John began to look forward to the hour alone in his room. He started to read in his father's Bible, noting with interest the comments written in the margins. The more John became unhappy with himself, the dearer the Bible became. Shame and guilt led him to cry out for forgiveness. He could hardly believe that the Lord would have mercy on him, for he had ignored and despised his father's pleadings. Thankfully, the worse John felt about himself, the more he turned to God's Word, and the more he cried out for mercy. The Holy Spirit showed him the beauty of the Savior, and there, finally, John found the peace and joy his father had always told him about. For the rest of his life, John kept his promise to his father, and spent an hour alone in his room—with God.

QUESTIONS

- What did John's father ask him to promise him?
- What are some things John did in his room?
- What are some things he thought about?
- How were John's friends a disappointment to him?
- Why did he begin to love the Bible?

THINK

- Why did John continue to spend an hour alone in his room every day?
- Do you spend time alone with God?
- What are some reasons we avoid spending time with God?
- Why is that foolish?

PRAYER

Help me to make time to spend
with Thee every day.

—29—

The Sleepless Night

The Lord is nigh unto them that are of a broken heart; and saveth such as be of a contrite spirit.

—PSALM 34:18

"I wish the clock wouldn't tick so loudly!" muttered Ruth. "I don't know why I can't sleep!"

She tossed and turned in her bed, doubling up her pillow one moment to make it higher, then throwing it aside, trying to find a comfortable position. "I did not steal; I didn't do anything wrong!" she said to herself.

Usually she fell asleep soon after lying down, and slept so soundly that it seemed to her that the night only lasted a few minutes. This time, however, she had listened to the footsteps of her brothers and sisters as they went to their rooms, had heard her father wind up the old clock in the hall, and had heard her mother's voice hushing the baby. All was still now in the house, except the ever-ticking clock, and yet she could not sleep.

Shall I tell you what troubled Ruth, so that the normally comforting sound of the old clock now bothered her so much? Ruth had committed a sin. The little boy who sat next to her in school had a couple of new storybooks which he refused to show her. She had caught glimpses of the colorful covers when he opened his desk, but when she asked again and again if she could please look at the books, Matthew said, "No!"

Ruth wondered what the stories were about and what the pictures looked like. Why did Matthew have to be so selfish? She thought about it so much that she broke the tenth commandment and coveted—she wished to have Matthew's books for herself.

After the children had gone home, the teacher had locked the schoolhouse door and left for home. Ruth lingered behind, talking with Katie Waters, a lively, cheerful girl who was afraid of nothing. Ruth had an idea. She asked Katie to climb in the back window with her.

"Sure, I'll do that," answered Katie casually, "but why do you want to do that?"

"I'll show you when we get in," replied Ruth.

Raising the window with little difficulty, she helped Katie climb in. Then she scrambled in after Katie. Ruth led the way to Matthew's desk.

"Look," she said, pointing to the beautiful books. "I want one of those. Matthew wouldn't let me look at them today. I don't know why he brings them to school if he doesn't let anyone else look at them," pouted Ruth.

Katie frowned.

"If you take one, Katie, and give it to me, then we can both say we didn't do it, when the teacher finds out and makes a fuss about it," prodded Ruth.

Katie looked at the books. They were beautiful hardbound children's books, with brightly colored pictures. "Ruth, if you had only wanted to play a trick on Matthew and just hide one for a while, I'd do it, but stealing is another thing. I don't steal."

"But who would find out, Katie? We could hide it in our barn, and we could read in it every day after school. Matthew is so selfish, he doesn't deserve to have the books!" Ruth added angrily.

"Don't you know, Ruth?" whispered Katie. "God will know it. I'm not taking those books. I'm getting out of here."

Ruth shut the desk after giving the books another longing look. Katie quickly climbed out of the window, and Ruth caught up to her as she left for home. "Please, Katie, don't tell anyone, ever, about this!" Ruth pleaded.

"Of course not," promised Katie. "I won't tell a soul. I won't even think about it again."

Ruth could not say the same. She thought about it all the rest of the day. "I don't see why I feel so bad about it," thought Ruth. "I didn't steal. I didn't do anything wrong. Matthew's books are still safely in his desk."

Now, in the darkness, listening to the ticking of the old familiar clock, Ruth did not feel as though she were innocent. What was she supposed to do? She thought that she should ask God to forgive her, but that would mean admitting she had sinned. "No, no!" she thought, "I didn't steal!"

But as the night dragged on, and Ruth became more agitated and nervous, she began to cry. She was guilty; deep down she knew it. Suddenly she remembered a verse she had heard recently, "For as he thinketh in his heart, so is he" (Proverbs 23:7). God saw her heart, and in His eyes, she was a thief. Not only was she a thief, but she had coveted and then had tried to make her friend a thief too. No wonder she could find no rest! She knew that only by asking forgiveness could she find rest.

She got out of bed and knelt down. "God, I'm so sorry," she began. Then the whole story came pouring out, along with tears and sobs. Wiping her tears away, she climbed back into bed, and with a deep sigh, drifted off into a sweet sleep.

God looks deeper than our outward behavior. We cannot convince God that keeping His commandments outwardly means that we are without sin. "As he thinketh in his heart, so is he" means that because we have sin in our hearts, we are condemned before God. We need our hearts renewed in order to please God. Confess your sin and guilt before Him, and He will make you clean. "Purge me with hyssop, and I shall be clean: wash me, and I shall be whiter than snow" (Psalm 51:7).

QUESTIONS

- Why couldn't Ruth sleep?
- Why was Ruth angry at Matthew?
- What did Katie refuse to do?
- Why did Ruth tell herself she had done nothing wrong?
- What verse did she remember? What did it mean?
- Why could she finally sleep soundly?

THINK

- What lesson did Ruth learn?
- Have you ever felt guilty even when you didn't physically do anything wrong? What did you do about it?
- In what way did Katie show courage?
- Do you refuse to join in doing wrong?

PRAYER

Keep me from sin—in thought, word, or deed.

—30—

The Story of Emilia

Then shall ye call upon me, and ye shall go and pray unto me, and I will hearken unto you. And ye shall seek me, and find me, when ye shall search for me with all your heart. And I will be found of you, saith the Lord.

—JEREMIAH 29:12–14

I want to tell you the true story of a little girl named Emilia. Her parents were godly people who taught Emilia by words and example what a blessed thing it is to be a Christian. Emilia thought often about what she heard and longed to become one of God's children. One morning, when she was only six years old, her anxiety became so great that she went to her mother to talk about her soul. She cried and said over and over, "I want Jesus to forgive me. I'm sorry I ever sinned against Him. He has always been so good to me. I'm sorry that I've sometimes argued with my little sister."

Emilia's mother told her once again about the blessed Savior, who is able and willing to save all who repent of their sins and give themselves to Him. But Emilia's distress continued. Day after day, she would come to her mother in tears because of her sins. Once she said, "What a wicked sinner I am! I want to belong to Jesus. But Christ sees me, and He knows I want to be His child."

Another day, she said, "The anger of God is terrible. I long to be in Jesus' arms, and my heart is full of sorrow because I am not a Christian." She then knelt and prayed with her mother, and afterward said, "What shall I do? I feel so awful! My crying will do me no good."

Emilia kept thinking that if she had come to Christ long before, then He would have received her, but now she said she had lived to be six years old already, and had not given her heart to Jesus all that time when He had been so ready to love her and forgive her. It seemed to her that such great ingratitude might never be forgiven. In her prayers, she would repeat many of the Bible promises, such as, "Suffer little children, and forbid them not, to come unto me: for of such is the kingdom of heaven" (Matthew 19:14).

Emilia would pray very often during the day, for she said she wanted to tell God how she felt. She felt that she was a very great sinner, and she wondered if Jesus would forgive her because she was so wicked. People might have been surprised at this, for she was considered a "good little girl." She was afraid to lie or to disobey her parents; she was kind and polite. Yet she felt that her heart was dreadfully wicked because she had not loved God. This was her burden.

She liked to go off alone to pray. "Lord Jesus, help me not to listen to Satan, who wants to destroy my soul. Help me to listen to Thee. Thou hast promised, 'Those that seek me early shall find me' (Proverbs 8:17). Fill my heart with Thy love."

Emilia was alone praying by herself one day, when she was able to give her heart to the Lord Jesus Christ. Such light and comfort came into her heart that she could not describe it. She jumped around the room, clapping her little hands for joy. She always remembered the very spot in the living room where she was kneeling. As she grew, she discovered more and more what a dear precious Savior and loving friend Christ is. She learned that even though she was a sinner, the Lord never tired of blessing her. She gladly served Him all her life and was a great blessing to many people, young and old.

Children, do you love the Lord Jesus Christ? If not, you remain in great danger! Flee to Christ, as little Emilia did. This little girl was not disappointed, and you won't be either when you go to Him. "Now therefore hearken unto me, O ye children: for blessed are they that keep my ways" (Proverbs 8:32).

QUESTIONS

- Why was Emilia distressed?
- Why did Emilia think God wouldn't forgive her?
- Can you remember a promise Emilia prayed?
- What changed? Why?

THINK

- Was Emilia a bad girl? Why did she feel so wicked?
- What did Emilia learn about God?
- Are your sins forgiven?

PRAYER

Show me what lives in my heart.
Cleanse me from all my sin.

Bearing
Fruit

—1—

A Student Artist Learns a Lesson

And we know that all things work together for good to them that love God, to them who are the called according to his purpose.

—ROMANS 8:28

Our heavenly Father deals with His people somewhat like the painter in this story dealt with his pupil. The student artist produced a beautiful picture which was admired by all. His young heart swelled with pride. He laid aside his palette and paints and sat daily before his easel, admiring the work of his hands.

One morning, however, he found, to his horror, that his canvas had been scraped clean. Gone was his masterpiece; only smudges of paint remained. He wept and shouted in anger and disappointment.

A little later, the master appeared in the studio. "What happened to my beautiful painting?" cried the student. "Who could have done such an awful thing?"

The master was silent a moment as he looked kindly into his pupil's tearstained face. Then he said, "I did this."

"What!" the young man exclaimed. "Why? It was my best painting ever!"

"I have done this for your benefit," the older man explained. "That painting was ruining you."

"How? It was so good! I was so proud of it!" moaned the student.

"Exactly. In the admiration of your own talents, you were losing your love of the art itself. Now take up your pencil and your paints, and start again."

The young man sat stunned as he thought about his master's words. Shame rolled over him. How vain and proud he had been! As his anger disappeared, his heart was filled with thankfulness and admiration for his wise teacher. He dried his tears, picked up his pencil, and produced a masterpiece. If it were not for this harsh test, this young man's talents would have been hindered and stunted by his sinful pride. He never forgot what his master taught him that day.

Children, remember this valuable lesson. Sometimes, like Jacob in the Bible story when he faced troubles, we think that "all these things are against me" (Genesis 42:36).

But if we are asking the Lord to bless us with eternal life, then He will work all things for our good. Sometimes things seem to go all wrong, and it seems that God has forgotten us, but if we are His children, then He will never forget us. We may not understand His ways while we live on this earth, but in heaven everything will make sense, and we will finally see that God's ways are best.

QUESTIONS

- Why was the student artist pleased?
- What happened to his painting?
- Who did this? Why?
- Why was the student eventually thankful for this?

THINK

- Why does God send trials to His children whom He loves?
- What are some things to remember when sad or painful things happen to us?

PRAYER

Humble me before Thee.

—2—

The Glass Factory

But he knoweth the way that I take: when he hath tried me, I shall come forth as gold.
—JOB 23:10

George Whitefield once told this story. "When I was at Shields, I went into a glass factory. Watching carefully, I saw several masses of burning glass in various shapes and sizes. The workman took a piece of glass and put it into a furnace. It was heated and then removed. The man placed it into a second furnace for a second heating, then a third. I questioned, 'Why do you put this piece of glass through so many fires?'

"The workman answered, 'Sir, the first fire was not hot enough, nor the second. That is why we put it into the third furnace, which is the hottest. The intense heat of that furnace will make it pure and transparent!'"

Just as the glass had to be heated to a very high temperature, so God's people must be "tried by fire" to burn out all their impurities. "Behold, I have refined thee, but not with silver; I have chosen thee in the furnace of affliction" (Isaiah 48:10).

QUESTIONS

- Where did George Whitefield go? What did he see?
- What question did he ask?
- What was the answer?

THINK

- What does it mean to be "tried by fire"?
- Why must God's children be tried by fire?

PRAYER

Make me pure so that I may reflect Thy image.

—3—

A Godly Woman

By this shall all men know that ye are my disciples, if ye have love one to another.

—JOHN 13:35

At least a hundred years ago, on one of the coldest days in February, a little boy stood peering into a shoe store window in New York City. He was barefoot and shivered in the cold. Just then, a lady rode up the street in a beautiful carriage drawn by a fine, black horse. She saw this little boy and noticed his bare feet and ragged clothes. Immediately, she ordered the driver of her carriage to stop. The richly dressed woman stepped down from the carriage and went quickly to the little boy.

"Little boy, why are you looking in that window?" she asked gently.

"I was asking God to give me a pair of shoes," answered the boy simply. "I don't have any boots. They didn't fit me anymore, so my brother is wearing them now. I'm glad for him, though," he added quickly.

The lady smiled and took the little boy's cold hand. She led him into the store. If the salesclerks were shocked to see a wealthy woman holding a dirty, ragged little boy by the hand, they did not dare to show it. The owner of the shoe store hurried to be of assistance.

"Mrs. Wilson! It's good to see you! How may I help you?" he asked politely, as if it were a common thing for dirty little boys to be led into his store by wealthy patrons.

"Would you please send one of your clerks to buy a dozen pairs of warm woolen socks for this poor child?" she requested with a smile, handing him some coins.

"Certainly, ma'am! John, go and do as the lady asks!"

"Now," continued Mrs. Wilson, "would you please bring me a basin of water, some soap, and a couple of towels?"

"Yes, ma'am, I'll get them right away!" answered the shopkeeper.

When he brought the basin of warm water, Mrs. Wilson asked the overwhelmed little boy to sit in a chair. He looked at his ragged clothes and then at the beautiful chair and stammered, "I don't think I should sit there, ma'am."

Mrs. Wilson turned her gaze to a salesclerk standing nearby. Quickly, he placed a towel on the chair so it would not be soiled by the boy's dirty clothing. The little boy gingerly sat down. Then, to everyone's astonishment, Mrs. Wilson removed her gloves, knelt down, and washed the little boy's feet. Then she dried them with a towel. By the time she had finished, the clerk named John had returned with the socks. He handed them to the woman. She took one of the pairs and put them on the little boy's feet. Guessing what she would request next, the shopkeeper brought a pair of beautiful leather boots, which Mrs. Wilson put on the boy. She got up, smiled at the boy, and said, "I hope you feel better now."

Speechless, the boy looked at the socks and the boots and then at the woman. He could think of nothing to say. Mrs. Wilson, however, did know what to say. "Do you have any brothers or sisters?" she asked. "You said you gave your old boots to your brother."

"Yes, ma'am, I have two brothers and two sisters. And a mother!" he added with pride.

Mrs. Wilson smiled, her eyes twinkling. "Would you like to go shopping for them? Should we keep it a surprise, or do you think they would like to come along?" She paused, thinking. "You know, I think they would like to come along. Would you please show me where you live? Then we can get acquainted and all go shopping together. What fun that will be!"

The astonished little boy looked up at her with tears in his eyes. In complete amazement, he asked, "Arc you God's wife?"

Children, perhaps this makes you smile. We know that God does not have a wife. But do you understand why this boy asked this question? What did Jesus do for His disciples? He washed their feet. Whom did Jesus help and love? Weren't they often the poor and despised? The little boy actually gave Mrs. Wilson a beautiful compliment. Christians are called to be like Jesus, or Christlike. The little boy noticed that God and the lady belonged together. Do you belong to God? Can others notice by your actions and your lifestyle that you belong to God?

QUESTIONS

- Why was the boy looking in the shop window?
- Why did the boy hesitate to sit on the chair?
- What shocking thing did Mrs. Wilson do with the basin of water? Why was it shocking?
- What did she suggest next?
- What question did the astonished boy ask her?

THINK

- Would the clerks have been polite to the boy had Mrs. Wilson not been with him? Why or why not?
- Why did the boy think Mrs. Wilson might be God's wife?
- How was this a compliment to her?
- Can you think of ways you can help a needy person?

PRAYER

Give me a heart of kindness and generosity.

—4—

The Storm and Its Lessons

The Lord *is thy keeper.*

—PSALM 121:5

A severe thunderstorm was raging one night. Two little girls were tucked in their beds, but they were not sleeping. The flashing of the lightning and the rolling of the thunder frightened the children, and they hid their faces under their blankets. The girls' mother was still up. The children heard her singing one of her favorite songs from the Psalter:

O God, our help in ages past
Our hope for years to come;
Our shelter from the stormy blast,
And our eternal home![2]

"Mommy!" cried one of the girls, "Aren't you afraid? How can you sing when the storm is so loud and scary?"

"My dear little girls," said their mother, kissing their cheeks, "how can I be afraid when I know that God is here? He takes care of us, and nothing can hurt us without His will. The lightning can do nothing except what God wants it to do. So don't be afraid; just try to think about the fact that you are safe in God's care. He will care for you and me."

The girls' mother opened their Bible and read a few verses out of Psalm 91: "He that dwelleth in the secret place of the most High shall abide under the shadow of the Almighty. I will say of the Lord, He is my refuge and my fortress: my God; in him will I trust" (vv. 1–2).

It wasn't long before the girls were sound asleep, comforted with the thought that God was watching over them.

2. Psalter 247:1 is based on Psalm 90.

QUESTIONS

- Why were the girls afraid?
- What was their mother doing?
- Why was she not afraid?

THINK

- Do thunderstorms frighten you? Why or why not?
- Who are the only safe people in the world? Why?
- Are you one of them?

PRAYER

Be my refuge. Keep me safe in
Thy secret place. (See Psalm 91:1.)

—5—

"Boy Wanted"

This book of the law shall not depart out of thy mouth; but thou shalt meditate therein day and night, that thou mayest observe to do according to all that is written therein: for then thou shalt make thy way prosperous, and then thou shalt have good success.

—JOSHUA 1:8

Ben read the notice posted in the window of the nice-looking country hotel. "Boy wanted," it said.

"I wonder if I could get a job here," thought Ben. "I must do something to earn money, or how will poor Mother be able to live? I guess I'll go inside and ask about it."

So Ben went in. It was the first time he had ever been in a barroom. The place looked neat and clean, and there were no drunken men about. But the smell of the place was sickening, and Ben's heart sank at the thought of living in such a place.

The keeper of the house was a good-natured, pleasant-looking man. In payment for his services, the man offered Ben a little room to sleep in as well as the tips he could make by holding the horses of travelers who stopped to get a drink and by doing little jobs for them. In return for these privileges, Ben was to make himself generally useful about the place, and if the innkeeper was away, he was to pour drinks from the glittering bottles for anyone who could pay for them.

"Well, now," said the innkeeper, "you have heard what I want you to do. Are you ready to begin work?"

"Give me a few minutes to think it over," said Ben, "and I'll make up my mind."

"Well, you may think about it, but I can get plenty more boys if you don't like it," exclaimed the innkeeper gruffly. He was surprised that Ben did not take the job right away.

Ben said nothing more but went out to the pump to get a drink of water. Then he sat down on a grassy bank to think the matter over. "What would Mother think of my working in a place like this? I think I would make a lot of money, but would she even want the money I made in this way? And what would God think of it? Doesn't it say somewhere in the Bible that a curse will be on the one who helps his neighbors get drunk?[3] If I get used to selling liquor to others, it probably won't be long before

3. See Hab. 2:5

I end up drinking myself. No, I just can't work in a place like this," decided Ben, and he returned to the tavern.

The innkeeper stood on the porch. "Well, son, what do you think of my offer?"

"I cannot take it," answered Ben bravely. "I need work very badly, but I cannot do this sort of work. God would not like it, my mother would not like it, and I wouldn't like it myself. I am afraid that I might end up becoming an alcoholic. I'm sorry, sir, but I just cannot do it."

Ben walked away, leaving the innkeeper wondering why the boy would walk away from such a well-paying job. But there was another person who understood him very well. This gentleman had driven up in a carriage to inquire the way to the next town just as Ben had given his answer to the innkeeper. He was very pleased with Ben's courage and willingness to follow God in spite of the consequences. He quickly caught up to Ben and invited him to take a ride in his carriage since he wished to have a talk with him.

Ben climbed in, and the gentleman said, "My son, I honor you for refusing to work in a bar, and that is why you will be just the boy for me. I want a helper in my store whom I can trust, a boy who is faithful to God, to his mother, and to his own conscience. That is clearly the kind of boy you are and the kind of boy I need."

The man offered Ben a good wage, and Ben went home to his mother that day as happy and thankful as a boy could be. Together they thanked the Lord for His protection, guidance, and care. "But whoso looketh into the perfect law of liberty, and continueth therein, he being not a forgetful hearer, but a doer of the work, this man shall be blessed in his deed" (James 1:25).

Ben had a difficult choice to make. Certainly, the offer of a good job was a real temptation, for his need for money was great. But this boy took the matter to the Lord, and the Lord richly rewarded him. We also face temptations. There are choices we must make to sin or to flee from sin. Our hearts are naturally inclined to sin, so fleeing from sin is not something we can do on our own. We must turn to the Lord for help like Ben did in this little story. God will certainly help us if we ask Him. Now you must remember that there is not always a quick solution as in this story. Think of those in other countries who are tortured, imprisoned, and even killed for choosing God's ways. Is that because God doesn't bless them? No, their blessing is received in their hearts; they are filled with the love and peace that come only from God. God's people here on earth certainly suffer, but through the Holy Spirit living in their hearts, they rejoice as they suffer for Christ's Name's sake. They know that their lasting reward awaits them in heaven. "Blessed are they that do his commandments, that they may have right to the tree of life, and may enter in through the gates into the city" (Revelation 22:14). They know that one day they will be forever with the Lord, whom they love so dearly.

Do you love the Lord Jesus enough to suffer and even die for Him? Would you be willing to give up everything you own and even be separated from those you love for the sake of Jesus? Ask the Holy Spirit to cleanse your heart from sin and to fill you with His love.

QUESTIONS

- Why did Ben want a job?
- What job did Ben first apply for? Why didn't he take it?
- Who overheard Ben as he explained why he couldn't accept the job?
- What job did the man offer Ben?

THINK

- Would you have taken the first job? Why or why not?
- Could God have blessed Ben at the first job? Why or why not?
- Why was the second job better?

PRAYER

Help me to live according to Thy commandments.

Johnny Christie

Stand therefore, having your loins girt about with truth, and having on the breastplate of righteousness.

—EPHESIANS 6:14

Two boys were in a classroom by themselves. One of them, who was named Johnny Christie, desired to walk in God's ways. The other boy, named Sandy Dawson, had no thought or care about God. Sandy had brought some fireworks, and he thought it would be great fun to set them off while the teacher was gone. When the teacher heard the bang and discovered the two boys in the classroom, he was angry with both of them. He first questioned Sandy.

"Sandy, did you set off those fireworks?" he asked.

"No, sir," answered Sandy.

"Johnny, was it you who did it then?" asked the teacher. Johnny refused to say yes or no. So the teacher gave him a severe punishment for being, as he thought, both disobedient and stubborn.

At recess, when the two boys were together, Sandy Dawson asked Johnny, "Why didn't you just say you didn't do it?"

"Because there were only two of us in the room. If I said I didn't do it, it would have been obvious that one of us was lying."

"Then why didn't you say it?" persisted Sandy.

"Because you had already said you didn't do it, and I didn't want to accuse you of lying."

Sandy was stunned. He also felt guilty. Johnny had been willing to take the punishment for him in order to avoid accusing him of sin.

As soon as recess was over, Sandy went right up to the teacher and said, "Sir, I can't stand it that Johnny was punished instead of me. I told a lie. I was the one who set off the fireworks. Johnny had nothing to do with it. I'm sorry, sir," he said with tears in his eyes.

As the teacher listened to Sandy, he thought about his own guilt in punishing Johnny wrongfully. He had simply assumed that Johnny was guilty. His conscience bothered him, and his eyes filled with tears too. He put his arm around Sandy's shoulder, and together they went to Johnny's desk. While the class listened in amazement, the teacher said, "Johnny, Sandy and I ask for your forgiveness. We were both wrong."

Everyone was very quiet. Johnny began to cry, for after all, it is hard to take a punishment you don't deserve. But he smiled through his tears at his teacher and at Sandy as he said, "Of course I forgive you!"

The entire class learned lessons that day that cannot be taught from books. They saw what it means to confess and to forgive. The children never forgot that day. Especially Sandy thought of that day as a turning point in his life. The teacher used the opportunity to teach the children about the punishment that Jesus took instead of His people. He urged the students not to ignore the Savior, but to flee to Him while they were still young.

"Remember now thy Creator in the days of thy youth, while the evil days come not, nor the years draw nigh, when thou shalt say, I have no pleasure in them" (Ecclesiastes 12:1).

QUESTIONS

- What did Sandy do?
- Why were both boys punished?
- Why didn't Johnny answer the teacher's question?
- Why did Sandy confess the truth to the teacher?
- Why did the teacher feel guilty?
- Why did Johnny cry?
- What lesson did the whole class learn that day?

THINK

- How would the story be different if Johnny had become angry with Sandy or with the teacher?
- Are you obedient to your parents and teachers? What do you do when you have been disobedient?

PRAYER

Teach me to be like Jesus in all I say and do.

—7—

Always Tell the Truth

Lie not one to another, seeing that ye have put off the old man with his deeds.

—COLOSSIANS 3:9

"Billy, don't go near that sandpile," warned his mother.

"But why not, Mommy? It looks like so much fun!" Billy was four years old and just learning that the world was bigger than his yard.

Billy's mother lifted him onto her lap and looked into his sparkling eyes. "Billy, if you go there, a bear will come and eat you up!"

The little boy looked frightened. "Bears?" he echoed. "I'm scared of bears. I won't go near the sand, Mommy."

A few days later, Billy was playing with his friend Alexander, who was a little older than he was.

"Billy, see that big sandpile over there? Let's go play in the sand!" suggested Alexander eagerly.

"No!" answered Billy firmly. "I'm scared of bears, aren't you?"

"What bears? There are no bears there! Who told you there were bears there?"

"My mommy told me," replied Billy. "And I'm not going near that sand or a bear will eat me up!"

Alexander didn't quite believe Billy, but he saw that Billy was convinced about the bears. Just then, their pastor walked by and asked, "How are you boys doing? Not arguing, are you?"

"Not really," answered Alexander. "But Billy said there are bears in the sandpile, and I don't believe him."

Billy's eyes filled with frustrated tears. "But my mommy told me there were bears there!"

The minister walked over to Billy and squatted down in front of him. "I'm sorry your mother said so, Billy, but the truth is, there are no bears there."

Billy began to cry, and ran home as fast as he could. "Mommy, Mommy!" he shouted. "Did you tell me a lie? Did you tell me that there are bears at the sandpile when there aren't any?"

Billy's mother wiped her hands on her apron and sat down on a kitchen chair. At once she saw the sin of what she had done. She had told a lie. "I'm very sorry, Billy. I should not have told you a lie. I wanted you to stay away from that sandpile because I was worried that you might get buried in the sand. I told a lie to scare you away from the sand."

"But Mommy, you told me that it is a sin to tell a lie!" Billy looked into her face, his eyes revealing his confusion.

"Yes, dear, I know," she answered, tears springing to her eyes. "Shall we ask Jesus to forgive me? I pray that I will never tell another lie."

They knelt down to pray. Just as Billy's mother was about to begin, Billy stopped her. "Wait! Let me pray. Maybe you won't tell Him the truth."

This pierced her heart like a dagger. She realized that her little boy had lost his confidence in her truthfulness. Sin always brings grief and pain, sooner or later. Billy did learn to trust his mother again, and the pain was healed because of Jesus' love and forgiveness. But sometimes sin's fruits are not so easily erased. Ask the Holy Spirit to make you clean and pure in the sight of God. Ask Jesus to forgive all your sins and to keep you from sin.

QUESTIONS

- What did Billy's mother tell him in order to keep him from the sandpile?
- What did Billy's friend tell him a few days later?
- Who told the boys the truth about the bears?
- What did Billy's mother realize?
- What did Billy say that hurt her?

THINK

- Was the lie Billy's mother told so bad? Why or why not?
- Do you always tell the truth?
- Why is it so important to always tell the truth?

PRAYER

Make me clean and pure in Thy holy sight.

—8—

A Conductor Learns a Lesson

Be kindly affectioned one to another with brotherly love; in honour preferring one another.

—ROMANS 12:10

A train was waiting at the station. The luggage was being loaded, people were hurrying back and forth with suitcases, and vendors were selling their wares. It was a busy place. A poorly dressed man made his way slowly to the train. He limped and walked with a cane. The conductor slapped him roughly on the shoulder and said, "Hey, Lame Leg, hurry up or we'll leave without you!"

The man climbed aboard with some difficulty. No one helped him. The last of the luggage was loaded into the luggage car. "All aboard!" called the conductor.

The man took a seat near the window. After the train had been traveling for a few miles, the conductor came by to check the tickets. Noticing the poor man, he said rudely, "Hey, it's Lame Leg! Hand me your ticket!"

"I don't have a ticket," said the man very quietly.

"No ticket!" exclaimed the conductor. "Pick up your briefcase then, and we'll put you off the train at the next station. We don't give free rides to beggars."

"I would advise you not to be so rude, young man," replied the stranger.

The conductor muttered something under his breath and went on to check the tickets of the other passengers. As he stopped at a seat near the back of the train car, a gentleman who had heard the conductor's conversation with the poorly dressed man asked, "Do you know who that person is?"

"No, sir. I've never seen him before."

"Well, that's Mr. Warburton, the president of this railroad. I thought you might like to know."

The conductor's face turned pale. "Are you sure?" he stuttered. "He doesn't look like a rich man."

"Oh, yes, it's Mr. Warburton alright. I know him very well."

The conductor was horrified. He was ashamed of himself. How terribly rude he had been! Hardly able to concentrate on his work, he finished collecting the tickets, and then quickly made his way to Mr. Warburton. Emptying his pockets of the record book, the tickets, and money he had collected, he gave them to Mr. Warburton. "I'm quitting my job, sir."

The president picked up the things the conductor had laid on the seat. "Sit down, young man. I would like to talk with you."

The conductor sat down nervously. When Mr. Warburton turned to look at him, the conductor saw no trace of anger.

"My young friend," began the president, "I'm sorry to see you act in such a rude manner. You have acted very badly. If you were to act this way to all people you don't like, you would do a great deal of harm to the company. I could tell the board of directors about your behavior, but I won't. If I did, you would lose your job, and you would probably have a hard time finding another. In the future, remember to be gentle and polite to all you meet. You cannot judge a man by the coat he wears, and even the poorest ought to be treated with kindness. Take your things. I won't tell anyone what happened. If you improve your behavior, you may keep your job. Have a good day, young man." Mr. Warburton stepped off the train, and the young conductor clumsily collected his papers. He had been taught a lesson that he would not soon forget. "Blessed are the meek," said Jesus in Matthew 5:5. "He that despiseth his neighbour sinneth: but he that hath mercy on the poor, happy is he" (Proverbs 14:21).

QUESTIONS

- What name did the conductor call the man with a cane?
- Why did he want to put the man off the train?
- What did the conductor learn about this man from another passenger?
- Why did the conductor say he was quitting his job?
- What did Mr. Warburton tell him?
- What lesson did the conductor learn that day?

THINK

- Do you ever call people names?
- Do you ever look down on someone who is different from you?
- How did Jesus treat people who were not accepted by others?

PRAYER

Help me to be kind and compassionate
to everyone, no matter who they
are or what they look like.

—9—

Be Ye Kind One to Another

We then that are strong ought to bear the infirmities of the weak, and not to please ourselves.

—ROMANS 15:1

"Stephen," called Mrs. Bennett as she stepped inside the door of her apartment. "I heard that Mr. Irving needs someone to work in his store. Why don't you go right now and talk to him about it?"

Stephen's face lit up at the prospect of getting a job. "That would be so nice, Mom, if we could find a way to make some more money. We sure need it!"

Mrs. Bennett nodded sadly. The death of her husband had made life very difficult for their family. She herself did what she could, sewing and washing clothes for other people. Stephen was the oldest of five children. The thought of sending him to beg in the streets of London frightened her. She had been asking the Lord to provide Stephen with a better way to earn money. Working for Mr. Irving seemed like a perfect job for her son.

She hummed as she made sure Stephen looked neat and clean before he set out. His clothes were well mended; he had only one set of good clothes. His boots were a bit too small and were worn through in the soles, but he was happy to have anything at all on his feet in this cold weather. A coat? He didn't even think of wishing for one. That would be a luxury!

With a goodbye wave to his mother and siblings, he set out, walking briskly to keep warm. He smiled, knowing his mother would gather the children around her and pray that the Lord would be with him. He added his own prayers to theirs. Five minutes later Stephen arrived at the store, but what he saw made his heart sink. There, waiting on the sidewalk in front of the shop, was a well-dressed boy. It looked as though he too wished to ask Mr. Irving about a job. Stephen sighed. Of course the nicely dressed boy would get the job. Who would hire a poor boy with patched clothes when a young man in nice clothes was available? Still, he had to try. Maybe Mr. Irving knew someone else who needed help.

Just then, a poor, shivering little girl crossed the street, and as she stepped onto the sidewalk in front of the two boys, she slipped on a patch of ice and fell in a puddle of melted snow. The well-dressed boy laughed rudely as the girl got up, water dripping from her thin, ragged clothes. She began to cry.

"My money! I had four nickels! Where are they?" she cried as she searched frantically for them in the slush with her bare hands.

Forgetting all about waiting for the shopkeeper, Stephen hurried over to the girl. "I'll help you. Don't cry," he said kindly.

Without hesitation, Stephen rolled up his sleeve and felt around in the dirty puddle. He came up with three coins. "Sorry, little girl," he said, "but I think the other one is lost."

"Then I can't buy the bread," wailed the child, "and Mama and the children will have no supper!"

Stephen knew what it was like to go hungry. He put his hand into his pocket and took out a few coins. He dropped the coins into his mittens. "Here," he said, holding them out to her. "These are for you. They're a bit big for you, but they'll keep your hands warm. If you carry your money in your mittens, you won't lose it so easily." He patted her shoulder like a big brother would do. "Go buy some supper for your family! Hurry, or you'll catch cold!"

The little girl looked at Stephen in amazement. Then she dried her tears, whispered her thanks, and hurried on her way. Quickly, Stephen washed off his hands with some snow and dried them on his pants. He frowned when he noticed his damp, rumpled clothes. He would never get this job now! But he was glad he had helped the little girl. She was around his little sister's age, and he had vivid memories of her crying with hunger.

The well-dressed boy had watched all this with a smirk. Now he laughed at Stephen. "Why did you even bother?" he scoffed.

Stephen looked up. He was about to answer when he noticed Mr. Irving. Oh no! Now he had no chance to go home and get cleaned up. But—Mr. Irving was smiling!

"What is your name, young man?"

The other boy gave his name, assuming that Mr. Irving would have nothing to do with Stephen.

"No, I mean the kindhearted boy who helped someone in need," interrupted the shopkeeper.

"Oh! My name is Stephen Bennett, sir," replied Stephen. "I—I came to ask about the job."

"And you shall have it!" exclaimed Mr. Irving.

How surprised both boys were! The well-dressed boy left, grumbling about unfair treatment. Stephen could not keep the smile from his face. "Really, sir? My clothes..."

"Never mind your clothes right now, Stephen. Your actions tell me far more about you than your clothes do, and I am pleased with your actions. God tells us we must love Him above all and our neighbor as ourselves. I have seen you do the second part. I hope to learn that you live the first part also."

Stephen was prepared to make a sacrifice in order to help someone in need. In our days, you can't buy a supper anymore for four nickels, but certainly there are still people who are needy. There are still many people who have less than others. There are children who are left out because of their disabilities or children who are shunned because of their looks or their accent or because their clothes are not the latest fashions. Are you kind? Do you help others? Or are you selfish? Do you look down on others? Do you think yourself to be better than others? What does God want us to do? Remember who has given you all the blessings you enjoy. Ask the Lord to give you a new heart so that you can "love the Lord thy God with all thy heart, and with all thy soul, and with all thy strength, and with all thy mind; and thy neighbour as thyself" (Luke 10:27).

QUESTIONS

- Why did Stephen need a job?
- What job was Stephen applying for?
- Who was waiting in front of the store? Why did that discourage Stephen?
- What happened to the little girl? Why was she crying?
- What did Stephen do for her?
- Why was the other boy laughing at Stephen?
- Why did Stephen get the job?

THINK

- How might the story have turned out if Stephen had ignored the little girl?
- What would you have done if you were Stephen? Answer honestly.
- How do you react when someone is laughed at?

PRAYER

Help me to love God above all
and my neighbor as myself.

—10—

A Painter's Life Saved

For my thoughts are not your thoughts, neither are your ways my ways, saith the Lord. For as the heavens are higher than the earth, so are my ways higher than your ways, and my thoughts than your thoughts.

—ISAIAH 55:8–9

Have you heard the story of Sir James Thornhill painting the inside of the cupola of St. Paul's Cathedral? He and another painter stood on some scaffolding since they were working high up. When Sir James had finished one of the compartments, he stepped back to get a full view of it. So intent was he on the painting that he forgot where he was. He did not hear the voice of the other painter calling out to him of his danger. He backed nearer and nearer to the edge of the scaffold. Another step and he would fall to his death!

Thinking quickly, his companion grabbed a wet paint brush and flung it against the wall, spattering the picture with unsightly blotches. Sir James flew forward in a rage. "What do you think you are doing?" he shouted.

Suddenly he realized what his friend had really done: he had saved his life! Knowing Sir James would rush forward to protect his painting, his friend had spared him from falling.

Just so, sometimes we get so absorbed with the world and are unaware of our danger. We walk farther and farther away from God and from safety and get nearer and nearer to perilous temptation. Then God in His great mercy "ruins our paintings" as it were; He seems to spoil something that we think is beautiful. We complain and murmur against His heavy hand. When the Holy Spirit shows us God's purpose and His love, however, we thank Him for keeping us from falling to our death. We realize that rather than ruining our wonderful life, God has been drawing us into His outstretched arms of mercy and grace. The very thing we thought was a disaster was actually meant for our salvation.

QUESTIONS

- Why were the two painters high up on the scaffolding?
- Why did Sir James not hear the other painter's warning?
- What did the other painter do? Why?

THINK

- What great danger are many people unaware of?
- In what way do we show that we are unaware of the danger?
- Are you saved from that great danger?

PRAYER

Keep me focused on Jesus Christ.

—11—

Polished Boots

Say not, I will do so to him as he hath done to me: I will render to the man according to his work.

—PROVERBS 24:29

"I was in Egypt some years ago," wrote the Rev. J. Stuart Holden,[4] "and held some services for the soldiers. One evening I got into conversation with a sergeant in a Highland regiment. He was just as bright and shining for the Lord as it is possible for a saved soldier to be. I asked him, 'How were you brought to Christ?' This is his story:

'There is a private in this same company who had been converted in Malta before the regiment continued on to Egypt. We gave that fellow an awful time. The devil had a willing accomplice in me, I confess, and I made that man's life a terrible burden for him. Of course, I did not realize then, as I know now, that I was in the devil's service as I persecuted that poor man. One wet and rainy night, he came in from his turn at sentry duty. He was very tired and very wet, but before getting into bed he got on his knees to pray. My boots were heavy with mud, and I hit him on one side of the head with my left boot and on the other side of his head with the right one, but he simply continued with his prayers. The next morning I was shocked to find my boots beautifully cleaned and polished by my bedside! This was that private's reply to my wicked treatment of him, and it broke my hard heart. That day I repented and turned from sin and Satan to God.'"

Instead of becoming angry, this meek soldier had responded with compassion to his persecutor, and in so doing, won him to Christ. He had learned to recognize an opportunity to be Christlike to his enemy. This is godly living: looking for opportunities not to hurt but to love our neighbors. What do you think might have happened if this soldier had responded with angry words and actions? What might

4. One of the scheduled passengers on the *Titanic* was J. Stuart Holden, eloquent preacher of St. Paul's Church in London. He had crossed the Atlantic many times to preach in the United States, often for Bible conferences. Less than twenty-four hours before the *Titanic* sailed, Holden's wife needed emergency surgery. The dilemma Holden faced was whether to fulfill his commitment to preach in the United States or to cancel his trip and remain with his wife. Trusting God's Word concerning his responsibility to his wife, he telegraphed the hosts of the conference that he would not be coming. Holden's *Titanic* ticket hung framed on his study wall for the rest of his life as a testimony to God's faithfulness and guidance.

have happened if this young private had thrown back those dirty boots? There would certainly have been trouble. Solomon said, "He that is slow to anger is better than the mighty; and he that ruleth his spirit than he that taketh a city" (Proverbs 16:32). Often our actions speak louder than our words. Sometimes we may not have an opportunity to speak, but we can still show our love by what we do. Jesus said, "Ye have heard that it hath been said, An eye for an eye, and a tooth for a tooth: but I say unto you, That ye resist not evil:[5] but whosoever shall smite thee on thy right cheek, turn to him the other also" (Matthew 5:38–39).

QUESTIONS

- Why did the soldiers make life miserable for their fellow soldier?
- What did this soldier do after a rainy night of sentry duty?
- What did the other soldier do to him as he prayed?
- What shock did the unpleasant soldier receive the following morning?
- Why did it break his heart?

THINK

- How would you have reacted to the mockery?
- Are you afraid to do right because of what people might say?
- How might the story be different if the soldier had responded in anger?
- Do you think it was easy or hard for him to clean those boots? Why?

PRAYER

Give me a heart filled with Thy love, so that
I may love others as Thou lovest me.

5. This has also been translated, "Do not resist an evil person"—that is, don't fight back.

—12—

A Little Girl's Question

The father of the righteous shall greatly rejoice: and he that begetteth a wise child shall have joy of him.

—PROVERBS 23:24

Mandy's mother was a dressmaker. If a woman wanted a new dress or a man wanted a new suit, she or he would go to the dressmaker's shop. The dressmaker would measure the person who needed the clothing and then sew the article of clothing for them. Sometimes, the dressmaker would go to the client's home if they requested this special service. One day, Mandy went with her mother to a wealthy woman's home in New York City. Mandy was five years old, a cheerful child, and a delight to everyone. This wealthy woman also liked Mandy at once.

"You have such a nice home," observed Mandy politely.

The lady smiled. "Would you like to see all the rooms in this house, Mandy?" she asked.

"Oh, yes! I would love that! My house doesn't have as many rooms in it as yours does!" exclaimed Mandy.

So they wandered from room to room, hand in hand, chatting like they'd known each other always. Mandy exclaimed over everything she saw. One of the rooms had an exquisite carpet. "You have such a nice house and such beautiful carpet," remarked Mandy. "It is like a palace. Jesus must come here very often. He comes to our house, and we don't have any carpet. Jesus comes here often, doesn't He?" questioned Mandy seriously.

The lady made no reply. She was surprised by the question and did not know how to answer.

"He comes here often, doesn't He?" repeated Mandy, tugging at the lady's hand.

The question had pierced the lady's conscience, and she answered honestly, "I'm afraid not, Mandy."

Mandy was very quiet after that. Soon afterward, she left with her mother. But God made use of Mandy's searching question. That evening the lady told her husband all about Mandy and the question she had asked. Mandy had assumed that such wealthy people would thank the Lord for His blessings and that He was a welcome guest in their home. The woman and her husband had to admit that they had taken their blessings for granted. They had not thanked God for anything, neither had they given Him their hearts. They were both convicted of the foolishness of living without the Lord. They began to read the Bible and went to church. The Holy Spirit blessed it to both of their hearts, and they became children of God. The Lord used the words of a little child to turn these people to Himself. "And a little child shall lead them," God's Word tells us in Isaiah 11:6.

QUESTIONS

- What was Mandy's mother's job?
- What did the woman show Mandy?
- What did Mandy ask the woman? Why?
- What was the woman's reply?
- How did God use Mandy's question?

THINK

- What dangers do we face when we have everything we want?
- Do you thank God for all the blessings He has given you?

PRAYER

Give me a thankful heart. Help me to use Thy blessings for Thy glory.

Courage to Pray

For whosoever shall be ashamed of me and of my words, of him shall the Son of man be ashamed, when he shall come in his own glory, and in his Father's, and of the holy angels.
—LUKE 9:26

Many years ago, a boy named Jamie got his first job on a wooden ship traveling from the River Nith[6] to Calcutta, India. He kept up his regular habit of kneeling for prayer before turning into his hammock for the night, not knowing he was doing anything unusual. An experienced sailor, Bob Shearer, who knew Jamie's parents, was watching the boy. He knew what to expect and wanted to protect the boy from the rude comments of the other sailors. At Calcutta, some additional sailors boarded the ship, one of them a mean, foul-mouthed villain named George. Bob was especially concerned about how George would treat Jamie, for the hardened sailor seemed to have no morals whatsoever.

Sure enough, the homeward voyage had scarcely begun when George, seeing young Jamie kneeling by his hammock, swore and shouted, "Lookee here! A youngster at his prayers!" Laughing raucously, he threw a shoe with excellent aim at Jamie's head.

With lightning speed, Bob grabbed George, hauled him up on the deck, and thrashed him thoroughly. His lip and nose bleeding, George slunk away, muttering oaths under his breath.

Jamie had not thought his prayers would cause so much trouble. He was clearly shaken by George's reaction and was afraid of the big man. The next night, Jamie decided to get into his hammock without kneeling. But Bob took Jamie by the heels and dragged him to his knees, saying, "Say your prayers like a man! Do you think I'm going to fight for a coward? Pray, or I'll need to thrash you next!"

This young boy was Sir James Anderson, commander of the *Great Eastern*,[7] who laid the first Atlantic telegraph cable. In this rough manner he learned a lesson he

---

6. The River Nith is located in southwest Scotland between Sanquhar and Thornhill.
7. In the 1860s, the *Great Eastern* was the only ship large enough to carry the single length of cable needed to build a telegraph line to span the Atlantic. The *Great Eastern* laid the successful Atlantic cable of 1866 with James Anderson as her captain.

never forgot: that no boy or man should, under any circumstances, be ashamed of his colors, his conscience, or his God.

QUESTIONS

- What did Jamie do every night before bed?
- What did George do when he saw Jamie praying?
- What did Bob do to George?
- What did Bob do when Jamie crawled into his hammock without praying?

THINK

- What lesson did Jamie learn?
- If you were in Jamie's place, would you dare to keep praying, or would you quit?
- How was Bob a blessing?

PRAYER

Help me never to be ashamed of Thee.

A Faithful Saying

All nations whom thou hast made shall come and worship before thee, O Lord; and shall glorify thy name.

—PSALM 86:9

Here is a story about something that took place at a mission school in South Africa. It shows how even young children may be drawn to Jesus and then may be used to draw others to Him. A man in Africa who cared nothing for religion was persuaded to send two of his children to the mission school. One of these children was an eight-year-old boy, and the other a girl of six. Since the station was some distance from their home, the children had to live at the house of the missionary. After they had been there some time, however, the father wanted the boy to help him in taking care of the cattle, so he went to the school to take him home. But the little boy had learned to love his teachers. He had also begun to love the lessons he was learning, and, above all, he was feeling his heart drawn to Jesus and was beginning to love Him. He did not want to go home and begged to stay. When his father asked the reason, he answered, "Because I can't learn anything like this at home."

"And what good things can a child like you learn here that you can't learn at home?" questioned the father impatiently.

"I have learned good things here like this verse: 'This is a faithful saying, and worthy of all acceptation, that Christ Jesus came into the world to save sinners; of whom I am chief' (1 Timothy 1:15). And, Father, I have learned who Jesus Christ is. He is the Son of God. I have learned that we are all sinners, and that He saves sinners."

These words of his little boy had such an effect on the father that he went home alone and left his boy at the school. In a few weeks he came back to the school a changed man. That one verse had drawn his heart to Jesus, and his soul was saved.

What about you? Is your soul saved?

You hear many more verses than this man did. He heard only one verse, and it was used for his salvation. What are you doing with all the verses you have learned? Do you treasure your Bible and read it often? Flee for salvation to the Lord Jesus Christ, the Savior of sinners. Will you go lost while those in faraway countries who hear only bits and pieces of the gospel enter into the kingdom of heaven before you? Ask the

Holy Spirit to cleanse your heart and to turn you from sin to God. That is the only way to true happiness and peace.

QUESTIONS

- Why did the boy and girl live at the missionary's home?
- Why did the father come to get the boy?
- What was the boy's response to the question about what he was learning?
- What effect did the boy's answer have on his father?

THINK

- What effect does the gospel have on you?

PRAYER

Give me a heart full of love to Thee.

—15—

My Daddy Is the Driver

Trust ye in the Lord for ever: for in the Lord JEHOVAH is everlasting strength.

—ISAIAH 26:4

Many years ago, a man boarded the train as he always did on his way to work. The train was behind schedule and was rushing along at an unusually high rate of speed in order to try to make up the time difference. The passengers were afraid that an accident might result, and many eyes reflected their fear. This man was also frightened and had visions of train wrecks in his mind's eye. Then he noticed a little girl of about four years of age walking down the aisle. He had seen her before and greeted her with a smile.

"Aren't you afraid to ride the train?" he asked.

"Sometimes I am afraid," admitted the little girl, "but not this morning!"

The man was surprised. "But everyone else is afraid this morning. Why aren't you afraid?"

"There's no danger," replied the little girl confidently, "because my daddy is the driver today."

Her father was the engineer, and she had such complete confidence in his ability to protect her that she felt perfectly safe and happy.

If that little girl could have such confidence in her earthly father, how much more should we trust the heavenly Father, who is "running the engine" of our lives? He orders and controls everything in heaven and on earth. If we are His children, then clouds and storms and darkness should not frighten us. Then He is our refuge and nothing can harm us while we are under His care.

QUESTIONS

- Why was the train going faster than usual?
- Why were the passengers afraid?
- What was the little girl's answer to the man's question?

THINK

- Why do we not need to be afraid if God is our Father?

PRAYER

Please adopt me as Thy child
and keep me safe forever.

—16—

Words Fitly Spoken

A word fitly spoken is like apples of gold in pictures of silver.

—PROVERBS 25:11

Many years ago, Mr. Nelson was a deacon in a church in central New York. He was a God-fearing man, and hardly a day passed that he did not speak to someone about their soul. In the same city lived Colonel Geoffrey, who took pleasure in ridiculing Christians and mocking the Bible. Mr. Nelson felt great concern for Colonel Geoffrey's soul, but he knew that anyone who had tried to speak to the colonel about God had made him terribly angry. Mr. Nelson, therefore, asked the Lord what he should do.

The Lord answered by providing him with an opportunity to visit Colonel Geoffrey on business. Mr. Nelson also talked with the colonel about eternity. He spoke earnestly about his need of a change of heart and the necessity of trusting in Christ alone for salvation. The colonel, however, would not listen. He began to curse and to swear. He insulted Mr. Nelson and scoffed at the words he spoke. Mr. Nelson sat quietly as Colonel Geoffrey shouted at him.

The meekness of the deacon surprised the colonel. "Why don't you say anything?" he asked.

"Colonel," replied Mr. Nelson, "I knew what I had to expect from you, and before I left home I prayed that God would give me the grace to bear it." His eyes filled with tears of compassion as he pleaded, "You are so unhappy! Won't you turn from your sin and flee to Christ? How can you die as you are and perish forever?"

Colonel Geoffrey was speechless. Overwhelmed at the love and meekness of this God-fearing deacon, he held his head in his hands and groaned, "Oh, Mr. Nelson, what a poor, miserable sinner I am!"

Mr. Nelson rejoiced inwardly. He read the Bible to Colonel Geoffrey. The very Book the colonel had mocked now became a precious source of hope to him. Mr. Nelson prayed with the colonel. The God whom this man had scorned as a figment of weak people's imaginations now became real to him as a righteous, holy, just, but also merciful God who blots out the sins of His people through the atoning blood of Jesus Christ.

The colonel humbly came to the Lord Jesus Christ, confessing his sins. Faithful to His promise, the Holy Spirit washed his heart clean. He was born again. Formerly, Colonel Geoffrey had ridiculed God, His people, and Christianity. Now he spoke often of his loving Father, his gracious Redeemer, and the blessed Holy Spirit. His greatest joy was to see others begin a new life in Christ. The people he had so despised became his dearest friends, but Mr. Nelson always held a special place in the colonel's heart.

QUESTIONS

- Who was Mr. Nelson?
- Who was Colonel Geoffrey?
- What did Mr. Nelson do after asking God for guidance?
- What was Colonel Geoffrey's response?
- How did Mr. Nelson react? How did this impact the Colonel?

THINK

- How might the story have been different if Mr. Nelson had become angry?
- Have you ever reacted to someone in a way that is not pleasing to God?

PRAYER

Use me for Thy glory.

Afraid of Lying

A false witness shall not be unpunished, and he that speaketh lies shall not escape.
—PROVERBS 19:5

One day, a little boy named Kenny had been sent on an errand by his father. He had stopped several times: to watch some boys playing in the park, to pet a beautiful dog, and to wander through the aisles of the general store on the street corner. At last he remembered that his father was waiting for the glue he had been sent to buy. He began to run as fast as he could to make up for lost time.

When he got near his home, one of his friends saw him and called out to him, "What's your hurry, Kenny?"

"I took so long getting my dad some glue, and now I'm afraid he'll be angry," Kenny answered when he caught his breath.

"Why don't you just say that the man in the store had to look a long time to find it?" suggested Kenny's friend.

"But he didn't have to look for it! It was right there on the shelf," said Kenny.

"So what? It would explain why you're late," reasoned his friend.

"But that would be a lie!" responded Kenny indignantly. "I don't tell lies! Even if I get the worst punishment my dad ever gave me, I won't tell a lie! My mom told me that lying leads to other sins. And the Bible tells me that no liars are allowed to enter heaven."

Kenny was right. Lying is a dreadful sin. David said in Psalm 51:6, "Thou desirest truth in the inward parts." Solomon said in Proverbs 12:22, "Lying lips are abomination to the LORD: but they that deal truly are his delight."

QUESTIONS

- What had Kenny's father sent him to do?
- What did Kenny do on his way?
- What did his friend tell him to say to his father?
- Why didn't Kenny want to lie?

THINK

- Do you think Kenny was punished when he got home? Why or why not?
- Do you think lying is worse than other sins? Why or why not?
- Do you tell lies?

PRAYER

Give me an honest heart that hates sin.

—18—

Holding Daddy's Hand

Thou wilt keep him in perfect peace, whose mind is stayed on thee: because he trusteth in thee.

—ISAIAH 26:3

Megan was a little girl, about six years old. At the end of the day, she loved to walk over to her father's office, which was only a few blocks away from her home.

"Come on, Daddy, let's go home," she would say.

"I'm so glad you came to walk with me," her father would say as he hugged Megan.

Today, Megan wanted to play a game. "Let's pretend I'm a blind girl, Daddy. I have to hold your hand, and you have to tell me what to watch out for."

So the bright blue eyes remained shut tight for the walk home, and Megan's daddy led her along. "Step up now, Megan," he would say, or, "Step down."

When they reached home, Megan excitedly told her mother what they had done. "Weren't you scared to walk around with your eyes shut?" she asked.

Megan beamed at her father and said, "Oh no, Mommy, I was holding Daddy's hand! I knew he would take good care of me!"

This is a beautiful illustration of what faith in God is and of the comfort it gives. God's children are perfectly safe when they put their hands in God's.

QUESTIONS

- What did Megan love to do?
- What game did she play with her father?
- Why was Megan not afraid to keep her eyes closed?

THINK

- How is this story a picture of faith in Jesus?
- Do you trust Jesus for everything?

PRAYER

Give me faith to trust in Thee
without questioning.

—19—

The Angels' Charge

The angel of the Lord encampeth round about them that fear him, and delivereth them.
—PSALM 34:7

Annie was a timid little girl. She did not like to be left alone in a dark room. One night after she had said her prayers, her mother helped her into bed. Giving her a good-night kiss, she was just leaving the room when she heard Annie say very softly, "Mommy?"

The mother went back to her little girl's bedside to see what she wanted. "The windows are making noises, and it sounds like someone's trying to get in," whimpered Annie.

"Well, I'll fix that," promised her mother. She put some wedges in the windows to stop their rattling. Then, sitting down by little Annie's bed, she said, "You're not afraid now, dear, when I am with you, are you?"

"No, Mommy. I don't mind the noise or feel afraid of anything when you're here with me."

"But Annie, your heavenly Father can take much better care of you than I can. He is with you all the time. Let me teach you a beautiful verse from the Bible. I want you to remember it and repeat it to yourself whenever you feel afraid. This is what it says: 'He shall give his angels charge over thee, to keep thee in all thy ways. They shall bear thee up in their hands, lest thou dash thy foot against a stone' (Psalm 91:11–12). Say this verse until you know it and can remember it as long as you live."

Annie repeated the verses several times, and then she said, "Mommy, you can go downstairs now. I'm not afraid anymore."

So her mother kissed her and went downstairs. Little Annie went to sleep repeating the verse she had just learned.

Are you ever afraid, children? You may always ask the Lord to protect you from sin and from danger. "For I, saith the Lord, will be unto her a wall of fire round about, and will be the glory in the midst of her" (Zechariah 2:5).

QUESTIONS

- Why was Annie afraid?
- Was she afraid when her mother was with her? Why not?
- What did Annie's mother tell her?
- Why was Annie no longer afraid?

THINK

- What do you do when you are afraid?

PRAYER

Be like a wall of protection around me.
(see Zechariah 2:5)

—20—

A Christian Lady

Six days thou shalt work, but on the seventh day thou shalt rest.

—EXODUS 34:21

A young lady named Deborah was on her way to a Southern plantation to begin her new job as a teacher. The plantation was a hundred miles away. Mr. Ramsey, the owner of the plantation, had come with several servants to meet her and accompany her home. They traveled pleasantly on through the luxuriant forests until night came on. The servants prepared a delicious meal, set up the tents for the night, and made sure Deborah had everything she needed.

The next morning was the Sabbath, the day of rest, but to her surprise, Deborah saw that Mr. Ramsey was preparing to travel farther. What should she do? He was her new boss. Should she disobey him? They were in the middle of the forest—would he leave her behind if she refused to go with him? It was easy to see that beneath his gentlemanly bearing lay a haughty spirit.

Deborah knew what she had to do. She asked the Lord for strength. Even though she was scared, she wanted to obey God and to leave the results with Him who rules over all.

"Mr. Ramsey," began Deborah, "do you realize that today is the Lord's Day?"

"Yes, I do," answered Mr. Ramsey. "But we have a long way to go, and I'd rather not waste a perfectly good traveling day sitting in the forest."

"I'm sorry, sir, but I cannot travel today," stated Deborah.

Irritated, Mr. Ramsey responded, "Well then, it seems I'll be going on without you."

"I am not afraid to travel alone," answered Deborah, "but I am afraid to break God's law. I will stay here until tomorrow, and then I'll continue."

The firmness of her answer struck Mr. Ramsey. He told a friend years later, "From that moment I felt a genuine respect for Deborah. I was sure that anyone who could remain so firm in her religious convictions would also remain trustworthy in other matters."

They did not travel that Sabbath day. They rested, and continued on Monday. Deborah became the teacher of Mr. Ramsey's children. They too grew to love and respect her. Mr. Ramsey entrusted her with other important tasks on the plantation as well.

We must also remain firm in obeying God. If all Christians would remain firm, even the world would respect them. Obeying God is not always easy. Sometimes the result is pain and suffering. But Jesus said, “If a man love me, he will keep my words: and my Father will love him, and we will come unto him, and make our abode with him” (John 14:23).

QUESTIONS

- Who was Deborah?
- What was her dilemma that Sunday morning?
- What did she do?
- What did Mr. Ramsey do?
- What was the result of Deborah’s choice?

THINK

- Would you have done what Deborah did?
- Is it easy to obey the Lord? Why or why not?

PRAYER

Help me to keep Thy commandments
because I love Thee.

—21—

Forgive Us Our Debts

Forbearing one another, and forgiving one another, if any man have a quarrel against any: even as Christ forgave you, so also do ye.

—COLOSSIANS 3:13

Two boys were playing together late one afternoon. All was well until Paul and Martin began to argue. They spoke very harshly to one another, using hurtful words, and parted in great anger.

When Paul got home, he went to his room and sat by the window, looking toward the west. He was feeling very unhappy as he thought about the quarrel he had just had with his best friend. He stared sadly out the window, watching the sun set. Suddenly these words came to his mind, "Let not the sun go down upon your wrath" (Ephesians 4:26).

The words startled him. "I can't stand this any longer," he said to himself. He stood up and left the room, telling his mother he'd be back in a few minutes. Paul crossed the street and rang Martin's doorbell. Martin answered the door, looking very angry. But Paul said quietly, "Martin, the sun is going down, and you know the Bible says we must not let the sun go down upon our wrath. I'm sorry for arguing with you and for saying those mean things."

Martin looked surprised, but soon a smile lit up his face. "That's okay, Paul. I'm sorry, too. You forgive me, and I'll forgive you, and we'll be friends again."

All of us can learn a lesson from this story, can we not? It is so easy to tell ourselves we did nothing wrong and that the fault is all with the other person. Sometimes it is so hard to say, "I'm sorry," isn't it? Ask the Holy Spirit to teach you true humility and true sorrow for sin.

QUESTIONS

- What happened to spoil Martin and Paul's afternoon?
- What verse came into Paul's mind as he watched the sun set?
- What did Paul do then?
- What was Martin's response?

THINK

- What lessons can we learn from this story?
- Have you ever had an argument with someone? What did you do about it?

PRAYER

Help me to apologize when I wrong someone.

—22—

Not Afraid

I will say of the Lord, He is my refuge and my fortress: my God; in him will I trust. Thou shalt not be afraid for the terror by night; nor for the arrow that flieth by day.

—PSALM 91:2, 5

A minister visiting the island of Sicily was caught in a sudden fierce thunderstorm. He sought refuge at the first cottage he could reach to get out of the heavy rain. He was kindly welcomed by the mother of the family of four children. After introducing himself and asking several questions, the minister asked the woman if she was afraid in this terrible storm. The thunder was very loud and the lightning flashed often.

Looking up with an expression of surprise, the woman answered, "And why should I be afraid? Am I not as safe in God's protection when the thunder roars as when the sun shines brightly?"

This woman was truly happy and secure. She was strong in her faith, giving all glory to God. Every true Christian is safe in God's protection. Are you safe for this life and for eternity?

QUESTIONS

- Why did the minister need shelter?
- What did he ask the woman?
- What was her reply?

THINK

- What do you do when you are afraid?
- Why does a Christian actually never need to fear?
- Then why are Christians afraid sometimes?

PRAYER

Keep me safe in Thy care.

—23—

The Powder Mine

Turn not to the right hand nor to the left: remove thy foot from evil.

—PROVERBS 4:27

Japan and Russia had been at war, but at last it was over. The soldiers and the sailors went back to their homes, glad that there was peace again. Two years went by. One night a little town on the coast of the Sea of Japan was awakened out of its sleep by a noise that seemed to shake the earth. Trees were uprooted, and houses fell in ruins. When the morning sun rose, ten men were found dead on the shore and 156 people were injured. It seemed as if the war had begun all over again. What had happened? What had caused this death and destruction?

During the war, the sailors had put powder mines out on the sea. These were explosives which floated on the water. When the big ships of the enemies struck them, they exploded, sinking the ships. One of these powder mines had obviously been floating on the waves for all this time. No ship had touched it; but at last, after two years, it touched the shore where it did its dreadful work.

Children, sin is just like that powder mine. Sometimes people commit sin and don't seem to be punished for it. The days and weeks and sometimes even years go by, and it seems everyone has forgotten about it. Verse 23 in Numbers 32 says, "Be sure your sin will find you out." It may be that no other person knows about a particular sin which you have committed, but the Lord knows it. He says, "For mine eyes are upon all their ways: they are not hid from my face, neither is their iniquity hid from mine eyes" (Jeremiah 16:17).

The best thing to do is to flee from sin. Ask the Lord to make you hate sin. Ask Him to give you a new heart. "Depart from evil, and do good; seek peace, and pursue it" (Psalm 34:14). Does your conscience tell you that you have sinned? Do your sins trouble you? Confess your sin to God, for He can wash away all your sin. He promises, "Let the wicked forsake his way, and the unrighteous man his thoughts: and let him return unto the Lord, and he will have mercy upon him; and to our God, for he will abundantly pardon" (Isaiah 55:7).

QUESTIONS

- What was the terrible noise during the night?
- What caused the explosion?

THINK

- How is sin like a powder mine?
- Do you think your sin is very bad? Why or why not?
- Why do we need to think about our sin?

PRAYER

Teach me to flee from sin to Thee.

—24—

Shaped for Heaven

That the trial of your faith, being much more precious than of gold that perisheth, though it be tried with fire, might be found unto praise and honour and glory at the appearing of Jesus Christ.

—1 PETER 1:7

I heard of a man who, during the Great Depression, lost his job, his wife, his home, and his money. He hung on tightly to the one thing he did have left—his faith. One day he stopped to watch some men doing stonework on a church. One of the workers was chiseling a triangular piece of stone.

He asked the worker, "What are you going to do with that?"

The worker replied, "See that little opening way up there near the spire? Well, I'm shaping this down here so it will fit in up there."

As the man walked away, he realized that God had spoken through that worker to explain the ordeal he was going through: "I'm shaping you down here so you will fit in up there."

Children, are there troubles and sorrows in your young lives? What do you do with them? Do you bring them to the Lord in prayer? The Lord sends us these trials so that we may turn to Him and seek Him not only for earthly things, but especially for the things of eternity. Do you love the Lord? If God were to take away all your earthly possessions and your family and friends, what would you have left? Is the Lord your Savior and Redeemer? If we belong to Him, we may thank the Lord for all the "shaping" He does in our lives, because it works to bring us closer to Him.

QUESTIONS

- What did the man lose during the Great Depression?
- What did he have left?
- Whom was he watching at work? What was one worker doing?
- What lesson did the man learn from this?

THINK

- Why does the Lord send trials?
- What do you do when you are sad or in trouble?

PRAYER

Cut away anything in me that
does not glorify Thee.

—25—

The Wounded Soldier's Return

When Simon Peter saw it, he fell down at Jesus' knees, saying, Depart from me; for I am a sinful man, O Lord.

—LUKE 5:8

One morning in 1863, a ship came to the wharf at Norfolk, Virginia, with an unusual load of passengers. The Union (Northern) and Confederate (Southern) armies fighting in the Civil War had agreed to exchange their sick and wounded prisoners. This particular ship was bringing back several hundred Union soldiers who had been held by the Confederates in prison hospitals. Many of these soldiers were in serious condition. There were not enough supplies and medicines to properly care for all these wounded men. Among these soldiers was a young man named Matthew, about eighteen years of age. He had been badly wounded and was weak and sick. His time in the prison hospital and the lack of proper clothing, medicine, and food had kept him from getting well. His body was covered in painful sores, and the wounds in his leg and arm did not seem to be healing.

Matthew had received word that his elder brother, William, would meet him at the wharf in Norfolk and take him home to Philadelphia. But Matthew was not as happy as you would expect him to be. When he got the message, he turned sadly to his friends and sighed. "William will not know me. He won't want to have me in his nice, clean home. I'll try to find a hospital, and the nurses will take care of me." Matthew wept as he looked at his filthy, ragged clothing and his thin, sore-covered body.

As the ship touched the wharf, a strong, well-dressed man hurried up the gangplank. It was Matthew's brother, William. He had been anxiously waiting for hours. Soon he was walking past the long row of beds, looking for his sick brother. Matthew was right—William did not recognize his brother. It was not pleasant to look at the sick men. They had sores, gray faces, filthy clothes, unwashed bodies, and dirty bandages.

Matthew's heart sank. "It's just like I thought. William doesn't know me, and he'd be disgusted if he did recognize me. Look how clean and dignified he looks. He will never want someone like me in his home."

William passed by the second time and still did not recognize his brother, but Matthew did not dare to say anything. Once more, William went carefully from soldier to soldier. He had almost given up hope of finding him, fearing that perhaps Matthew had died on the way home, but he tried a third time. He stopped by Matthew's bed, still not recognizing his own brother. Gazing sadly at Matthew's pitiful condition, he whispered compassionately, "Poor fellow!" He was about to turn away when a faint cry stopped him.

"William, don't you know me?"

In amazement, William turned and looked again at the thin figure on the bed. "My dear brother! Why didn't you say anything before?" Without waiting for an answer, William stooped and lifted his brother easily in his strong arms. He carried him, rags, filth, sores, and all, off the boat and into a carriage that he had waiting for him. His strength, his money, his house, his servants, and all he had were used to nurse Matthew back to health.

Children, what a beautiful picture this is of how the Lord Jesus saves His people. Jesus, the almighty, loving Savior, takes the filthy, stinking, sick, dying sinner in His arms and heals him. Just as William was happy to care for his dear brother, so Jesus loves to save sinners and make them His children. "And the Spirit and the bride say, Come. And let him that heareth say, Come. And let him that is athirst come. And whosoever will, let him take the water of life freely" (Revelation 22:17).

QUESTIONS

- Who were the passengers on the ship?
- Why was Matthew unhappy?
- Who came to meet him?
- Why didn't William recognize Matthew?
- What did William do when he realized it was Matthew?

THINK

- How is William a picture of Jesus?
- How are we like Matthew?

PRAYER

Wash away all my sins and make me Thy child.

Rock of Ages

There is none holy as the Lord*: for there is none beside thee: neither is there any rock like our God.*

—1 SAMUEL 2:2

A little girl named Dora, who had learned to know and love and trust in Jesus, was visiting her friend Mary. In the living room of Mary's house hung a large picture. It showed a rock rising up in the midst of a stormy sea. On top of this rock stood a cross. Clinging to this cross was a woman who had apparently just escaped the angry waves. She seemed exhausted, but she clung closely to the rock. At her feet the artist had painted the hand of someone still in the water, grasping a part of the ship that was sinking down amid the waves.

"Do you like the picture, Dora?" asked Mary's mother when she noticed the girl studying it.

"Yes, I do. What does it mean though?" asked Dora.

"The painting is called *The Rock of Ages*," volunteered Mary.

"That's right," smiled her mother. "It is intended to represent Jesus our Savior, to whom we must cling for salvation. You know how the hymn goes:

> Jesus, Lover of my soul,
> Let me to Thy bosom fly,
> While the nearer waters roll,
> While the tempest still is high.
> Hide me, O my Savior, hide,
> Till the storm of life is past;
> Safe into the haven guide;
> O receive my soul at last![8]

There's another hymn about clinging to the cross:

8. Charles Wesley (1707–1788).

Nothing in my hand I bring,
Simply to Thy cross I cling;
Naked, come to Thee for dress;
Helpless, look to Thee for grace;
Foul, I to the fountain fly;
Wash me, Savior, or I die."[9]

"Oh, yes, I know those hymns," answered Dora. But after a moment's hesitation, she added, "That rock isn't really like my Jesus, because when I cling to Him, He reaches down and clings to me too."

Dora had learned that her salvation did not depend on how firmly she clung to her Savior. Rather, her security was found only in Christ, who held her fast in His grip. He would never let her go, no matter how weak she might be. "In God is my salvation and my glory: the rock of my strength, and my refuge, is in God" (Psalm 62:7).

QUESTIONS

- Describe the picture Dora saw in Mary's house.
- What did the picture represent?
- Why did Dora say the rock wasn't like her Jesus?

THINK

- What lesson had Dora learned?
- Do you know what Dora meant?

PRAYER

Teach me to cling to Thee.
Hold tightly to me and never let me go.

9. Augustus Montague Toplady (1740–1778).

—27—

Slander and Gossip

An hypocrite with his mouth destroyeth his neighbour: but through knowledge shall the just be delivered.

—PROVERBS 11:9

There was once a minister's wife who had a very effective way of stopping a person from speaking slander or gossip in her presence. Whenever someone would say something unpleasant about someone else, she would get her hat and coat.

"Where are you going?" the person would ask.

"I'm going to visit the person you mentioned and ask if what you said is true."

People became very cautious about speaking unkindly about anyone in her presence. Do you participate in gossip or slandering another person? It is a very serious sin. You must fight against it and stop it completely. Ask the Lord to help you and instead speak good things about others. Titus is directed by Paul to "put [his congregation] in mind to be subject to principalities and powers, to obey magistrates, to be ready to every good work, to speak evil of no man, to be no brawlers, but gentle, shewing all meekness unto all men" (Titus 3:1–2).

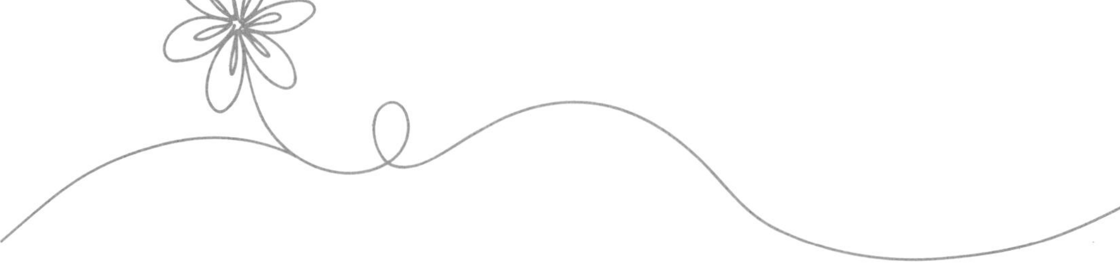

QUESTIONS

- What would the minister's wife do when someone said something unpleasant about another person?
- Why did she do this?
- What was the result?

THINK

- Do you ever say anything unkind about someone else?
- Why is this a serious sin?

PRAYER

Help me never to say unkind or untrue things about another person.

—28—

The Bird and the Butterfly

And the Lord said, Simon, Simon, behold, Satan hath desired to have you, that he may sift you as wheat: but I have prayed for thee, that thy faith fail not.

—LUKE 22:31–32

A woman was taking a nap one summer afternoon while staying at the home of a friend in the country. After a while she was awakened by a strange noise, as if something were knocking against the window. She got out of bed to find out what it was. There, behind the curtain, on the inside of the window, was a butterfly beating frantically at the window. What was the cause of its fear? Outside the window was a large sparrow. It sat on the outside window ledge pecking on the window, trying to get at the butterfly. The butterfly did not see the glass nor know that it was there. But it knew that the sparrow was its enemy, and it was afraid that any minute the sparrow would eat it up. The sparrow did not see the glass either. It was expecting any minute to get hold of that tasty butterfly and eat it up.

And yet the butterfly was just as safe as if it had been miles away from that sparrow. That thick pane of glass was between it and its enemy, and that bedroom was a safe haven for it.

So it is with us when we come to Christ Jesus for refuge and abide in Him. We are perfectly safe then. His presence and His power are between us and every danger. He says to us then, as He did to Abraham, "Fear not.... I am thy shield" (Genesis 15:1).

QUESTIONS

- What woke the woman from her nap?
- Why was the butterfly beating against the window?
- What did neither the butterfly nor the bird see?

THINK

- How is this story a picture of safety in Jesus?
- Are you safe in Jesus?

PRAYER

Be my safe place.

—29—

The Living God

My soul longeth, yea, even fainteth for the courts of the Lord: my heart and my flesh crieth out for the living God.

—PSALM 84:2

At family devotions one evening, little Mary looked anxiously up at the face of her father. He was no longer living close to the Lord, and his heart had grown cold. Evening devotions were now merely form and custom, not a time of communion with God.

Mary's lips quivered as she asked, "Dad, is God dead?"

"No, my child. Why do you ask that?" responded the father.

"Well, Dad, you never talk to Him now like you used to," she replied sadly.

These words burned in the father's heart until he repented and was forgiven by his gracious heavenly Father. "The father of the righteous shall greatly rejoice: and he that begetteth a wise child shall have joy of him" (Proverbs 23:24).

QUESTIONS

- What question did Mary ask her father?
- Why did she ask that question?
- What was the result?

THINK

- Are you close to God or far away from Him? How do you know?

PRAYER

Draw me very close to Thee in love.

—30—

An Apology

Put them in mind... to speak evil of no man, to be no brawlers, but gentle, shewing all meekness unto all men.

—TITUS 3:1–2

There once was a man named Mr. Douglas, who was a Christian. He had been talking to Mr. Jameson, who was not a Christian. Mr. Jameson had a bad temper. He was angry at Mr. Douglas because of something Mr. Douglas had said to him. Mr. Jameson was very surprised when Mr. Douglas knocked at his door.

"What do you want?" he asked roughly.

"Mr. Jameson, I have come to apologize for what I said to you earlier today. I am sorry it offended you. I've come to ask for your forgiveness."

Mr. Jameson was speechless. This was not what he expected. He had been prepared to shout and scold. After a moment he said, "Of course, I forgive you, Mr. Douglas."

After Mr. Douglas had left, Mr. Jameson sat down in a chair. "What a strange man this is!" he thought to himself. "Everybody knows what a bad temper I have. It was probably not easy for him to come and apologize. He probably thought I would shout at him. But still he came to see me! I wonder if it's because he's a Christian. Maybe Christianity is a good thing after all. I'd better look into it."

And Mr. Jameson did look into it. He began to attend church services and to read his Bible. He learned to pray. The Holy Spirit began to work in his heart and renewed him. He learned, by God's grace, to control his temper and to be patient and kind. "If any man among you seem to be religious, and bridleth not his tongue, but deceiveth his own heart, this man's religion is vain" (James 1:26). "He that is slow to anger is better than the mighty; and he that ruleth his spirit than he that taketh a city" (Proverbs 16:32).

QUESTIONS

- Which man had the bad temper?
- Why was Mr. Jameson angry at Mr. Douglas?
- Why did Mr. Douglas come to see Mr. Jameson?
- Why was Mr. Jameson surprised at this?
- What effect did it have on him?

THINK

- What does your anger say about you?
- Read James 1:26. What does it mean?

PRAYER

Give me a heart that is loving and kind.
Keep me from sinful anger.

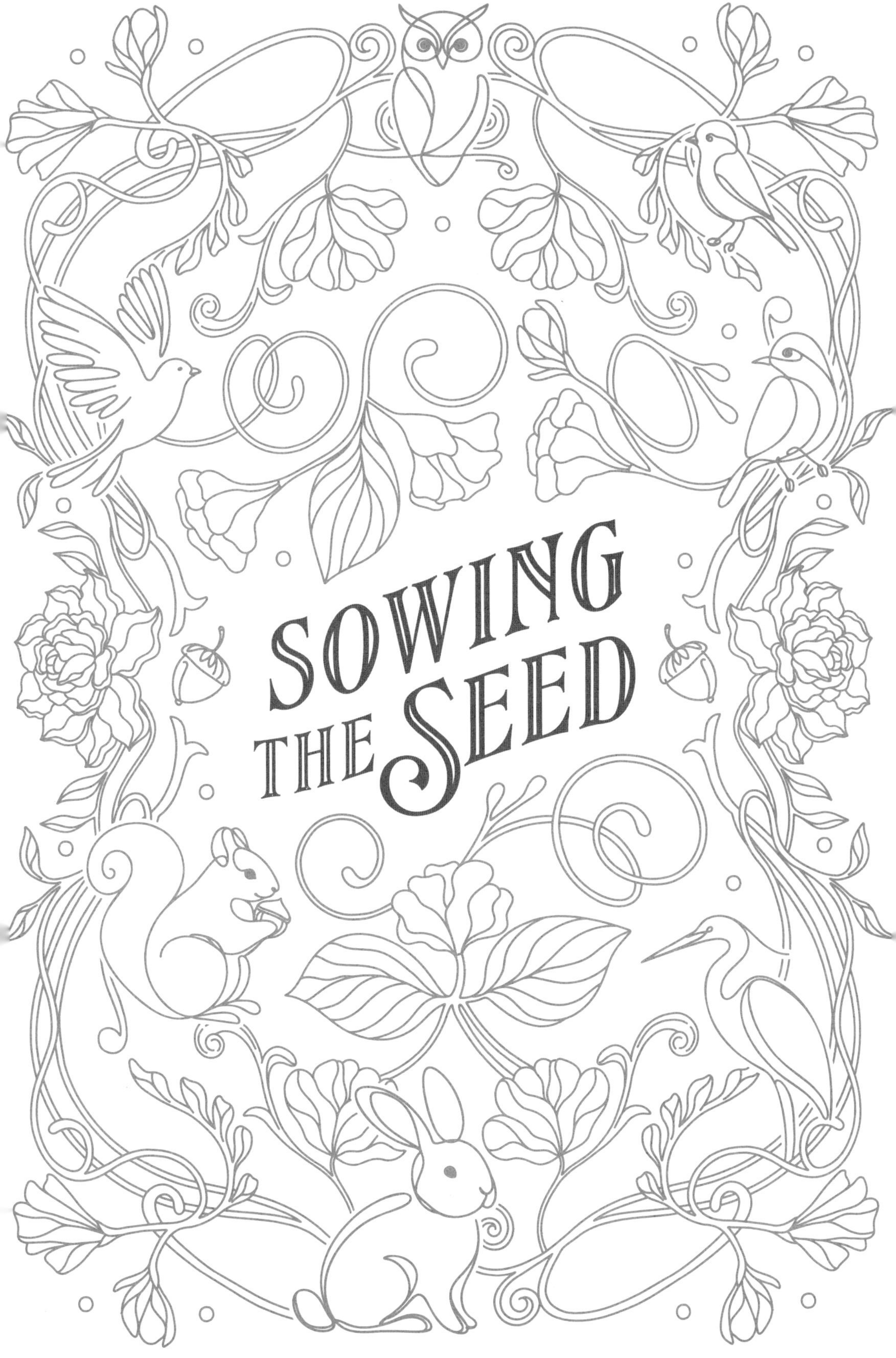
SOWING
THE SEED

—1—

A Faithful Pastor

Is it not to deal thy bread to the hungry, and that thou bring the poor that are cast out to thy house? when thou seest the naked, that thou cover him; and that thou hide not thyself from thine own flesh?

—ISAIAH 58:7

On one of the bitterest mornings of a cold New Hampshire winter, a devoted servant of God in a seacoast town was bundling himself up for a morning walk.

"What?" exclaimed his wife in alarm when she saw him pull on his gloves. "Are you going out today? It is much too cold! You had better stay safely inside by the fire."

"I really have to go visiting in the east part of the county, dear," the pastor replied calmly. "It has been a long time since I have visited the families there. I have meetings all day tomorrow, and I may not have another opportunity for weeks."

"But it is so cold!" fretted his wife.

"Then it might be even more important that I go today just because it is so cold," countered the pastor. "They are more likely to be at home." He smiled at her. "Don't worry, dear. I'll dress warmly."

He filled a bag with tracts and little books as well as some packages of tea, sugar, flour, and even some butter and jam. With a cheery good-bye to his wife, the minister stepped out into the cold. He plodded steadily through drifts of snow, over fences, and through the woods until he came to the farthest edge of the county. In a little house down in the valley lived an aged couple, far from any neighbors. They were both in their eighties and had been kindly and cheerfully supported by people in town for years, but the extreme cold this week had kept people from coming out to see them. Their firewood had been used up, and the poor old man was out in the intense cold, feebly trying to cut down an old willow tree, which had shaded the house for many years. His wife was inside, in bed, since it was too cold to do anything else. There was no wood with which to build a fire to warm the house.

The pastor greeted the old man, took the axe from his tired arms, and soon chopped down the old tree. After he had cut a few pieces of wood and collected some dry branches, he went inside and built a cheery fire. Then he went back outside and cut up enough wood to last for at least a week. He felt no cold, for the exercise warmed him. The old woman got up and made a pot of tea. Together the three of them sat by the fire and warmed themselves. The old man took down a worn black Bible from the shelf. The minister read a chapter and prayed with them. Before he left, he placed some tracts on the table, and with words of encouragement and kindness, the pastor went on his way.

All through that cold day, he went from house to house among the poor of his community, giving comfort to those who mourned, quiet encouragement to the sick, and kindness and love to all. The minister shared news of the neighbors with those he visited. The hearts of those who had food and clothing in abundance were softened to give to those in need. Strong men went out to lend a hand to the poor and weak. Woodpiles were replenished and empty pantries now had shelves with a variety of food. Those who had extra clothes or blankets gladly gave to those who were cold and needy.

Did the faithful pastor suffer from the cold? Not at all! He came home with a song on his lips and thanksgiving in his heart. Paul said, "I have shewed you all things, how that so labouring ye ought to support the weak, and to remember the words of the Lord Jesus, how he said, It is more blessed to give than to receive" (Acts 20:35).

QUESTIONS

- Why was the minister going out on such a wintry day?
- What was the old man trying to do?
- What did the minister do for the elderly couple?
- How did the minister's actions impact others?
- What blessing did the minister receive?

THINK

- What would have happened if the minister had stayed home?
- What can you do to help someone?

PRAYER

Help me to use my hands, eyes, ears, and strength to help someone today.

—2—

Doing God's Work

I beseech you therefore, brethren, by the mercies of God, that ye present your bodies a living sacrifice, holy, acceptable unto God, which is your reasonable service.

—ROMANS 12:1

In the year 1665, the city of London, England, was struck by the bubonic plague, also called the "Great Plague" or the "Black Death." That year the summer had been exceptionally hot. Though no one knew it at the time, the plague was spread by rats, which hosted disease-carrying fleas. In seventeenth-century London, there was no safe system for getting rid of the garbage and waste. People would simply throw their trash into the streets. This, combined with the extreme heat that summer, was the perfect environment for rats. The slum areas of London were hit especially hard by the plague.

The plague was a dreadful disease. Thousands of people became sick and died. Though some tried, no doctors could cure it or do anything to relieve the suffering of the patients. Since it was very contagious, people would leave the city if they could to try to avoid catching this terrible sickness.

The poor were very badly hit by the plague. The authorities in London decided on drastic action to ensure that the plague did not spread. Any family that had one member infected by the plague was locked in their home for forty days and nights. The home was chained shut from the outside and a red cross was painted on the door to warn others of the plight of those in the house.[10]

The rich left London to try to escape the fast-spreading disease, but this was not an option for those who lived in the slums. They did not have relatives or friends outside of London with whom they could stay. They had no choice but to remain in London, and they were afraid.[11] Death was everywhere. Businesses and schools were closed; churches were empty. Every day more people became sick, and every day more people died. Reverend Thomas Vincent was a minister who lived in London during this time. The king of England had dismissed him as a pastor because he would not follow the king's rules. Instead, he found a job teaching school. When he heard that

---

10. http://www.historylearningsite.co.uk/plague_of_1665.htm
11. Ibid.

the plague had reached London, he closed his school and asked God to show him how to help the people. After some time in prayer, he believed God was calling him to visit the sick and dying, telling as many people as he could about the Lord Jesus Christ. Most of the other ministers had left the city or died from the plague. Reverend Vincent's family and friends were shocked and frightened when he told them he was going to stay in London. They tried to persuade him not to do this. They told him it was much too dangerous and that he should not willfully expose himself to such great danger. However, Reverend Vincent refused to go. He believed the Lord wanted him to remain in London. Reverend Vincent did not know if he would live or die, but he trusted God, who could protect him from danger if that was His will. Daniel's three friends, Shadrach, Meshach, and Abednego, did not know whether they would die in the fiery furnace, but it was more important to them to obey God. Just like those brave men, the Reverend Vincent would rather obey God and die than live being disobedient. He was willing to die doing the Lord's work, because he loved the Lord and wanted others to be saved.

Therefore, he stayed in London. He preached in some of the churches. You can imagine how hungry the people were for God's Word. They did not know if they would live another week to hear another message, and they listened eagerly. Many people knew they were not ready to meet God. Crowds of people flocked to the churches. Every day of the week, Reverend Vincent visited the sick, reading the Bible to them, and speaking to them and their families about preparing for eternity.

There were dying people all around him. Because of his love and concern for their souls, Reverend Vincent worked tirelessly bringing the gospel to homes where others feared to go. Families locked in their homes certainly appreciated the visits from this courageous, loving servant of God. Only the Lord knows how many people were saved through this determined man's efforts.

During that fearful time, nearly 70,000 people died of the bubonic plague in London. Seven members of Reverend Vincent's own family died, but the Lord spared His faithful servant. He was never sick even one hour during that time. He trusted in his God and did the work the Lord had called him to do. God protected him from danger. "Whoso putteth his trust in the LORD shall be safe" (Proverbs 29:25).

QUESTIONS

- What sickness struck London in 1665?
- What caused it?
- Why did the poor remain in the city?
- What did Reverend Vincent do when he learned about the plague?
- Why were his friends and family frightened when they learned of his decision to stay in London?
- Why was he not afraid?
- Why did so many people come to church?

THINK

- Was it foolish of Reverend Vincent to remain in London? Why or why not?
- Can you think of people in the Bible who were kept safe in danger?
- Does everyone who trusts God escape all dangers or even death?

PRAYER

Give me a heart that follows Thee without fear.

—3—

A Shy Woman

Not by might, nor by power, but by my spirit, saith the Lord of hosts.

—ZECHARIAH 4:6

Many years ago, a murderer sat in his cell in prison, repeating to himself the sentence pronounced by the judge: "You are to be hanged by the neck until you are dead, and may God have mercy on your soul!"

However, there were no tears in the prisoner's eyes and no repentance in his heart. His heart grew harder as he repeated those words, and he cursed both God and man. Ministers had visited him with gospel messages from the Word of God, but he despised their words and told them to leave him alone.

"But you are condemned to die!" argued one of the ministers. "In a few weeks you will enter eternity. How can you stand before God with your sins unpardoned?"

"That's my business," growled the prisoner. "Go away!"

The story of the bitter prisoner made its way into the newspaper. Among those who read the story was a shy Christian woman. As she read it, her eyes filled with tears, and she felt a desire to visit this man. "But I can't do that!" she told herself. "I have never been to a jail in my life, and I wouldn't know what to say. I do wish I could say some kind words to the poor man."

Every day, the desire to visit the murderer grew stronger in her heart. She believed the Lord wanted her to visit this condemned criminal. Asking for the Lord's strength and guidance, she made her decision. She went to her garden and picked a beautiful bouquet of flowers. With a pounding heart, she approached the prison. A guard showed her the way to the prisoner's cell. Banging on the bars of the little window, he called, "There's a woman here to see you!"

After a moment the prisoner's scowling face appeared behind the bars of the window. The woman's courage fled, and her voice failed her. She couldn't think of anything to say. As she handed the flowers to the man, the tears flowed down her cheeks. "For you," she whispered. She stood for a moment gazing at the prisoner, and then, because she still couldn't think of anything to say, she turned and left.

The sight of the flowers and the weeping woman had a strange effect on the prisoner. It brought to his memory thoughts of his godly mother, who wept when he left home in rebellion. All these years, the prisoner had locked away these memories, for he did not want his conscience to be bothered with thoughts of God and his mother. Now the Holy Spirit used these things to lead him to Himself.

While the woman was on her way home, thinking she had failed in her purpose, God was working repentance in the heart of this hardened criminal. Falling on his knees, he cried out, "Oh God, be merciful to me a sinner!"

God, who gave this prayer, also answered it for the sake of His Son, Jesus Christ, and the prisoner found forgiveness and peace in Christ. The shy woman's tears and kindness had melted his heart, and he was led like a little child to the Lord Jesus.

QUESTIONS

- What was the prisoner's crime?
- What was his sentence?
- What was his reaction?
- How did the shy Christian woman learn about the prisoner?
- Why did she hesitate to visit him?
- What did she take with her?
- What did she say and do when she saw the prisoner?
- What effect did this have on him?

THINK

- Why do you think the woman felt she had failed in her visit?
- What can we learn from this woman?

PRAYER

Help me to be obedient to Thee
even when I am afraid.

—4—

A Father Taught by His Child

Out of the mouth of babes and sucklings hast thou ordained strength because of thine enemies, that thou mightest still the enemy and the avenger.

—PSALM 8:2

Eric's parents had held family worship ever since they had married, and when Eric was born, they had included him too. The little boy began to love this time of the day, and when he was not able to be there because of illness or some other reason, he was very sad. Even when it seemed he was too young to understand, family worship was his favorite part of the day. Eagerly, he listened to his father's deep voice as he read from the Bible, and solemnly, he knelt by his chair for the prayer that followed.

One morning, when Eric was still very young, his father was in a big hurry. He was late and had an important business meeting to attend. He rushed through breakfast and skipped family worship. Eric got off his chair and knelt down. His father continued putting on his coat. Eric got up and ran after him, pulling on his coat. "Papa, papa!" cried Eric. "Pray, pray!"

Stunned, Eric's father put down his briefcase and removed his coat. "Yes, little one, you are right. We must not forget God before beginning our day." His eyes filled with tears, for he was ashamed of himself. What kind of example had he set for his son? Must the Lord use a baby to teach him? Eric's father never forgot this simple but most important lesson.

Children, no one is ever too young to belong to Jesus. Little Eric began to love the Lord when he was only a baby. Ask the Lord to make you one of His children. Then you can serve Him all your life long.

QUESTIONS

- What time of the day was Eric's favorite?
- What did Eric's father forget one morning when he was in a hurry?
- What did Eric do?

THINK

- Can babies and children be saved? Why or why not?
- Are you saved? If yes, how are you serving God? If no, what are you doing about it?

PRAYER

Give me a heart that loves Thee,
so that I may serve Thee all my life.

—5—

The Convict

Then spake the Lord to Paul in the night by a vision, Be not afraid, but speak, and hold not thy peace.

—ACTS 18:9

Some time ago, as I was traveling by train in Vermont, I heard the clanking of chains. I was curious. Across the aisle from me sat a man who was obviously a sheriff, judging from his uniform. I asked him if he knew where the sound was coming from.

In response, he asked, "Do you see this young woman next to me?"

I looked past him and saw the woman he referred to. She looked at me without smiling. Her intelligent face was thin and pale, her brown eyes filled with sadness. The sheriff continued, "She is twenty-eight years old. A few weeks ago, she crossed the border from Canada and entered a village in the state of New York. Along with some rough young men, she broke into a store at night and robbed it. The store owner was badly injured in the attack and much of his merchandise stolen or broken. They were all sentenced to a long confinement in the state prison. My job is to transport her to prison. Because she has been very cooperative I have allowed her to remove the shackles from her feet and keep them in this satchel at my feet." He nudged the bag with his foot, and I heard again the unmistakable sound of chains.

I felt compassion for her. Her whole life had been ruined by a foolish sin committed in one fateful night. Some time later, we made a stop at one of the stations, and I saw the convict sitting on a box in a corner away from other travelers. The sheriff sat beside her. He did not speak to her but kept a sharp eye on her. I approached the sheriff, told him I was a member of the American Tract Society, and asked if I could give her some of our tracts.

"Certainly," he replied. "It may do her some good. I will tell the prison guards when we arrive that a minister gave them to her on the way, and then she will be allowed to read them." The sheriff turned to the young woman and explained, "This minister wants to give you something to read."

I handed her two little books and some tracts and told her I hoped they would be a blessing to her soul. To my great surprise, her face changed completely. Her eyes lit up, and a lovely smile brightened her face. It was as if she was being reunited with old friends. I wondered if perhaps she had read these at home in her teens or if she had been raised by godly parents who were now grieving over their wandering daughter. "Oh, these are beautiful books!" she exclaimed, tears filling her eyes. "I love to read! I have wanted something to read! I will most certainly read these books!" Then she added quietly, "I hope they will do me a great deal of good, sir. Are you really a minister?"

She seemed eager to hear once again the familiar but precious story of the Savior who died selflessly for sinners. She drank in the gospel, a sad smile on her tired face. I prayed with her, and she quietly thanked me.

How often the words and acts of Christian kindness fall upon a soul like raindrops in a desert! How eagerly this young woman responded to these godly tracts! I do not know what became of this young woman—I never saw her again—but I have always prayed that this brief conversation and the tracts given to her may have been used for the salvation of her soul.

Children, this is a nice story, but also a sad one. How different the life of this young woman would have been had she obeyed the gospel in her youngest years. How much pain she could have avoided had she turned to the Lord before she ruined her life. Do not put off your salvation! Do not push aside the warnings and invitations of the gospel. The Lord stands ready to save. Will you insult and anger Him with your refusal to obey? Turn to Him now, without delay. You will not be sorry. "Seek ye the Lord while he may be found, call ye upon him while he is near: let the wicked forsake his way, and the unrighteous man his thoughts: and let him return unto the Lord, and he will have mercy upon him; and to our God, for he will abundantly pardon" (Isaiah 55:6–7).

QUESTIONS

- Who was the prisoner?
- What was her crime?
- What was the sheriff's job?
- What did the author give to the prisoner?
- What was her reaction?

THINK

- Do you think the minister's words were a blessing to the prisoner? Why or why not?
- What lessons can we learn from this story?

PRAYER

Teach me to walk in Thy ways, starting today.

—6—

The Widow's Mite

And [Jesus] said, Of a truth I say unto you, that this poor widow hath cast in more than they all: For all these have of their abundance cast in unto the offerings of God: but she of her penury hath cast in all the living that she had.

—LUKE 21:3–4

At the anniversary of the London Missionary Society in 1829, the Reverend Dr. Dickson of Edinburgh told the following story.

"Once, when I was collecting contributions for the Scottish Missionary Society, I preached in Paisley. The next day, I was met by an old woman who was dressed in a faded, patched dress. She greeted me cheerfully. I asked her who she was. She answered, 'Sir, I heard you preach yesterday. I wanted to give something for the mission, but I have not had any work the last four days. God, however, has provided for me. He knows that I do not like to go to a missionary meeting when I have nothing to give, so I went to some friends and told them that you were requesting donations. One lady had just a halfpenny; others had several pennies. Altogether, I have collected nineteen and a half pennies. I am so glad that God heard my prayer and provided this money for me to give to the missionary society.'

"I appreciated those few pennies more than the large gifts received from wealthy people because of the cheerful spirit in which they were given. If, then, God has given you more than before, I ask you to do just like this poor woman of Paisley. This will not only encourage the Christian directors of the missionary society, but it will enable them to cheer the hearts of the millions of human beings who, except for your gifts and prayers, may never hear of the way to eternal life."

QUESTIONS

- Why couldn't the woman give her own money?
- What did she do instead?
- Why did the minister especially appreciate this small donation?

THINK

- Why do you think the woman wanted to give a donation?
- How important is mission work? Why?
- What can you do to help missionaries?

PRAYER

Bless and encourage missionaries all over the world. Turn many people to Jesus.

—7—

Betsy Brown

I have blotted out, as a thick cloud, thy transgressions, and, as a cloud, thy sins: return unto me; for I have redeemed thee.

—ISAIAH 44:22

The Reverend Worley lived in a New England village. He was a kind man who tried to help those in need, whether they belonged to his church or not and whether their needs were physical or spiritual. There was one woman in his neighborhood whom he very much wished to help. Her name was Betsy Brown. Betsy worked in a bar. She was a big, strong, loud woman who cursed and swore terribly. The Reverend Worley knew she needed the Lord's grace, but he had found no opportunity to speak to her. She did not attend church, and she avoided the Reverend Worley and his wife whenever she happened to meet them in town. The Reverend Worley was very concerned for Betsy's soul. He prayed for her and asked the Lord to give him an opportunity to bring her the gospel. He and his family and friends prayed earnestly that God would open some way for someone to reach this poor woman.

One day Betsy fell, spraining her knee very badly. The doctor told her she had to stay in bed to let it heal. She could not walk at all because of the pain. Betsy was frustrated and angry about her sprained knee. She fretted and fumed like a caged tiger. Since she lived alone, there was no one to care for her. A woman who lived a few houses away from Betsy came to help occasionally, but no one else dared to visit her.

After praying about it, the Reverend Worley decided it was a good time to visit Betsy. So one day, as Betsy sat alone, hungry and uncared for, there was a knock at the door.

"Come in!" she called.

To her great surprise, in walked the minister. He asked her kindly, "How are you today, Betsy? Do you have much pain?"

"Yes, it hurts all the time," admitted Betsy with a frown.

"Is there anything I can do for you?" asked the Reverend Worley.

"I don't think you know how to do anything except read the Bible and pray," snapped Betsy.

The minister did not answer but made a fire in the fireplace to drive the chill out of the room. Then he went to the kitchen and boiled some water for a cup of tea. He cut a few slices of the bread his wife had baked and found some butter and jam. As an extra surprise, he slipped a piece of chocolate onto the tray. When Betsy saw the tray with the delicious food on it and the piece of chocolate, the big strong woman began to cry. "I haven't been able to eat anything all day because I can't get up," she said tearfully. "I can't believe you would do this for an awful woman like me!" After she had wiped her tears, she continued, "I've had time to think while I was sitting here helplessly with nothing to do. I do not have any friends. Everyone is afraid of me. I am so lonely, but it is my own fault. After my husband died, I decided I did not need anybody's help, and especially not God's help. That is why I am the way I am. Nobody likes me—I do not even like myself! Why did you come to visit me? I have not been nice to you and your wife."

"Let me tell you of what Jesus Christ did for sinners," offered the Reverend Worley, "and then you will understand how easy it is for me to come and help you."

God graciously touched Betsy's heart. She listened with great interest while the minister talked to her about Jesus, the Savior of sinners. This was the first of many talks, which were the means of Betsy's salvation. What a change was made in Betsy Brown! She was led to see her sins and to repent of them. She was indeed "born again."

It seemed Betsy could not do enough in the service of her Lord. She quit her job at the bar. No longer did she utter oaths and curses, but her house rang with the sound of prayer and song. She became a "missionary" in the village, speaking to others and helping wherever she could. The Lord used her to reach people whom no one else could reach. "If the Lord can change me, He can change anyone," she would say. As gruff and unkind as she had been before, she was now loving and generous. God's people saw the change in her and rejoiced, and many lost sinners were led to Christ because of the miracle God had performed in Betsy. "Let the wicked forsake his way, and the unrighteous man his thoughts: and let him return unto the Lord, and he will have mercy upon him; and to our God, for he will abundantly pardon" (Isaiah 55:7).

QUESTIONS

- Whom did Reverend Worley want to help?
- Where did Betsy work?
- How would you describe Betsy?
- Why did she have to stay in bed?
- Why did no one dare to visit her?
- What did Reverend Worley do for Betsy? What was her reaction?
- Why was Betsy interested to hear about Jesus? What was the result?

THINK

- Why was Betsy unhappy?
- Why was kindness the best way to reach Betsy?
- What can we learn from this story?

PRAYER

Help me to be kind and loving to everyone,
even people who are unpleasant.

—8—

College Friends

In all things shewing thyself a pattern of good works: in doctrine shewing uncorruptness, gravity, sincerity, sound speech, that cannot be condemned; that he that is of the contrary part may be ashamed, having no evil thing to say of you.

—TITUS 2:7–8

In a graduating college class in the early 1800s, there were four young men who were close friends. After their graduation, each of these young men went their separate ways. None of them were Christians. Two of the four were very much opposed to Christianity, but God, in His great mercy, saved one of these rebellious men, so that now Donald loved the Bible he had despised for most of his life.

Donald also became concerned for the souls of his dear friends. He wrote to his friends, telling them of the joy he had found in serving the Lord. He wrote to them of the need to be born again. He urged them to think about eternity. Every day, Donald prayed for his friends. However, Donald's friends did not welcome his letters. One friend in particular called him a religious fanatic and told him he was ruining their friendship.

Instead of being discouraged, however, Donald continued to write letters to his friends. Repeatedly he wrote, but received only cold answers in reply. Continually Donald urged them to examine the Bible and to try to pray, to see if these things were true. Daily, Donald pleaded and wrestled with God for their conversion.

God heard Donald's prayers and blessed his labors of love. The friend who was most bitterly opposed to Christianity was the first converted. He cried out, "What must I do to be saved?" He asked Donald for his prayers. Eventually each friend found salvation in Christ alone.

These four friends all became ministers of the gospel. The three friends thanked God for Donald's persistent letters and prayers to God on their behalf.

QUESTIONS

- How many friends were there?
- How many were Christians at first?
- Whom did God save first?
- What did Donald do?
- How did his friends respond?
- What was the end result?

THINK

- How does this story show God's love for sinners?
- Are people who go to church more deserving of God's mercy than those who do not? Why or why not?
- What effect do you have on your friends?

PRAYER

Help me to point my friends to Jesus.

—9—

God Wants Our Best

And I say unto you, Ask, and it shall be given you; seek, and ye shall find; knock, and it shall be opened unto you. For every one that asketh receiveth; and he that seeketh findeth; and to him that knocketh it shall be opened.

—LUKE 11:9–10

What would you think of a boy who kept an apple until it was rotten before he tried to eat it? What would you think of a girl who kept a rose until it wilted and faded before she put it in a vase? What would you think of a man who bought a car and never used it until it was old and rusted? What would you think of boys and girls who waited until they were old before they began to seek the Lord?

There once was a girl named Margaret. She lived in the city of St. Louis where she had many friends and relatives. One day her mother became ill and had to be taken to the hospital. After a few days, Margaret's mother was allowed to go home, but a nurse came to visit every day to make sure she was all right. This nurse was a Christian. She knew that Margaret's family went to church and read the Bible, but when the nurse talked to Margaret about the Lord, the little girl said she would think about that when she was older. The nurse began to pray for the little girl. She asked the Lord for an opportunity to talk to Margaret about the need of being converted.

One day a beautiful bouquet of flowers arrived for Margaret's mother. Margaret thought it was lovely.

"May I bring them to Mommy now?" asked Margaret.

"Well, I think we had better not take them to her just now. They are so fresh, sweet, and beautiful. Let's keep them in the closet for a few days and then we'll bring them up to your mother's bedroom for her to enjoy," answered the nurse casually.

Margaret's eyes opened wide with surprise, and she looked at the nurse to see if she were joking. "Do you mean that?" asked Margaret uncertainly.

"Sure!"

"That's a bad idea!" shouted Margaret. "These flowers are from Aunt Grace, and she's my mother's only sister! She'll want to see them right away!"

The nurse smiled gently at Margaret and put her arm around the little girl. "You are right, Margaret. I think your mother should be able to enjoy the flowers when they are sweetest and freshest, and we will bring them up to her as soon as she wakes up from her nap. I wanted to teach you something, Margaret. Don't you think God should have your life when it is at its best? You are keeping your young life from Him when you do not seek Him. You say you will seek Him when you are older, but the best time to seek the Lord is when you are young."

Margaret thought often about the nurse's words. She saw that she was wrong in putting off trusting in Jesus. She realized she had been very foolish. Thankfully, she learned a lesson that day and began to seek the Lord from that day on.

QUESTIONS

- Where did Margaret live?
- What happened to her mother?
- Why did the nurse come every day?
- Why did the nurse begin to pray for Margaret?
- What did she suggest to do with the flowers?
- What was Margaret's response?
- What did the nurse explain to Margaret?
- What was the effect?

THINK

- Why is it a bad idea to seek the Lord when you are old?
- Why is it a good idea to seek the Lord when you are young?

PRAYER

Give me a heart to love and serve Thee today.

Protection through Providence

We having the same spirit of faith, according as it is written, I believed, and therefore have I spoken; we also believe, and therefore speak.

—2 CORINTHIANS 4:13

The still form of a little boy lay in a coffin, surrounded by mourning family and friends. A stranger entered the room and paused at the coffin to gaze at the boy. Tears streamed down his face. He turned and spoke to the little boy's grieving parents.

"You don't know me," he said, "but your boy was a messenger of God to me. Once I was working on a very high roof. I came down a long ladder and saw your little boy standing nearby watching me. He looked up into my face and asked, 'Weren't you afraid of falling when you were up so high?' Moreover, before I had time to answer, he laughed and said, 'Oh, I know why you weren't afraid! You asked God to protect you before you went to work this morning!'

"He assumed I was kept safe because I prayed, but he was wrong. I had not prayed; in fact, I never prayed. I will never forget your little boy. God used him to turn me around. I began to feel guilty for taking God's protection for granted. I had never asked Him for anything, nor thanked Him, and yet He had done so much for me. Then I began to think about my soul: certainly, I was not ready to meet God! I found a Bible and began to pray. After meeting your son, I never forgot to pray. I think of him every day. By God's grace, I will never stop praying until I meet your son in heaven."

QUESTIONS

- What question did the little boy ask the man on the ladder?
- How did the boy answer his own question?
- What effect did the question have on this man?
- Why did the man think of that little boy every day?

THINK

- Do you ask the Lord for His protection? Every day?
- Do you thank Him for His care? Every day?
- Do you think God cared for the little boy even though he died?

PRAYER

Thank you for Thy care every day.
Please take care of me today.

The Man Who Paid

Who his own self bare our sins in his own body on the tree, that we, being dead to sins, should live unto righteousness: by whose stripes ye were healed.

—1 PETER 2:24

About one hundred years ago, a Christian lady was spending the summer at the seaside. She would go and visit people in her neighborhood. In one of those summer cottages lived a boy named Matt who had Down syndrome. He could not read or write; he could not name any of the letters of the alphabet. Today there are educational programs managed by professionals for children with Down syndrome and other impairments. A century ago, however, people thought these children were not able to learn so they were not sent to school. Often they were seen an embarrassment to their families and considered a punishment from God because of some sin the parents had committed.

Miss Ella, as Matt called her, loved Matt and visited him often. She walked with him along the seashore or in the fields and tried to teach him something about God, heaven, and his own soul. Before the summer was over, Miss Ella discovered that the Holy Spirit had taught Matt that he was a sinner, and Matt was very distressed about it. She realized that the only way to comfort him was to tell him about Jesus who came to save His people from their sins (Matthew 1:21). But how could Matt understand these great things? Satan tempted Miss Ella to think that this was impossible. Many theologians could not fully understand these doctrines. How could Matt with his limited mind grasp these amazing truths? The Holy Spirit reminded Miss Ella "out of the mouth of babes and sucklings hast thou ordained strength" (Psalm 8:2). With this encouragement, she determined to try to teach Matt, praying for wisdom, patience, and the Lord's blessing.

Taking his hand gently in hers, she said to him one day, "Matt, I know that you are a sinner. Sins are the debts you owe to God. Now, when one man owes a debt to another man that he cannot pay, he must be put in prison for it.[12] God has a prison

12. Years ago, a debtors' prison was a place for people who did not pay their debts. Men, women, and even children were kept there until the debts were paid. Often, people lived their entire lives in prison because they had no way of paying their debt.

too, called hell. Nevertheless, although you cannot pay your debts to God, God has made a way that your debts can be paid. God has a dear Son, named Jesus, whom He sent all the way from heaven to pay for debts. If you ask Him to pay your debts, you will not have to go to God's prison. Jesus paid the debt by suffering and dying on the cross. Therefore, you must ask Jesus to forgive your sins. Then you will be free forever and live with Him in heaven forever after you die."

Matt listened with his eyes and ears wide open while the lady was speaking to him. When she was finished, he said with great earnestness, "Tell it again, Miss Ella, tell it again!" And she did. Repeatedly she told him the old, old story of Jesus and His love. Very simply, she told him of the Savior's redeeming love. She told him the story of His birth, His life on earth, His love for sinners, and His death and resurrection. God, by His blessed Spirit, helped Matt to take it in; he saw and understood the great love of Jesus in dying for his sins. This took away all his fear. For a while, he seemed to forget everything but God and his great love for Jesus Christ. Everywhere he went, Matt would tell people about Jesus, who paid the debt.

One day, as he sat by the seaside with Miss Ella, talking about Jesus, his heart seemed to burst with joy. He jumped to his feet, stretched his hands toward heaven, and shouted, "God and Man who paid my debt, Matt says, 'Thank you! Thank you!'"

From that time on, Matt never lost the joy that he found in Jesus his Savior. Not long afterward, he became sick and died. The last words he spoke as his dear friend, Miss Ella, sat at his bedside, were these: "God-Man who paid the debt, please come and take poor Matt to live with Thee forever!"

The love of Jesus is simple and powerful so that even a child with Down syndrome like Matt can understand it. No one is beyond the reach of God's power. God is almighty. He can save you. He is willing to save you and pay your debt of sin. Seek Him while you are young!

QUESTIONS

- Who was Matt?
- How did the Christian lady meet Matt?
- Why didn't Matt go to school?
- What did Miss Ella try to teach Matt?
- Why was Matt distressed?
- What did Miss Ella try to explain to him?
- What effect did this have on Matt?
- How did Matt express his joy and gratitude?

THINK

- Can you name three things you learned from this story?
- Has Jesus paid your debt?

PRAYER

Please pay my debt through the blood of Jesus so that I may live a life of thankful obedience to Thee.

—12—

IN THE SERVICE OF THE LORD

Also I heard the voice of the Lord, saying, Whom shall I send, and who will go for us? Then said I, Here am I; send me.

—ISAIAH 6:8

Long ago, a young man was converted. Not long after this, he felt called to the ministry. While he was studying, he decided to make himself useful. He used his Sundays and any other free time he had to try to do some good in a poor, neglected neighborhood. There was no church and no Sunday school in that part of the city, and no place available to hold services.

At last, he found an unfurnished house and rented the third story. He fixed it up and used it as a Sunday school meeting place.

Very few people came at first. However, he persevered, diligently visiting throughout the neighborhood, inviting people to come and hear the gospel. Earnestly, he prayed for the dew of God's blessing to rest on his labors. Attendance steadily increased until, finally, the room was crowded.

Then the young man went to work again to try to build a church in that neighborhood. By his efforts, the money was raised, and a sturdy stone church was built. Then a parsonage was built. A large congregation of the poor went regularly to worship God now. There was evidence in their daily lives that many had been truly converted from sin to God.

All around that church, dark homes were brightened. Many people who once lived in sin and misery now led happy, useful lives in God's service. All this good fruit was brought forth by God's blessing on the labors of that one faithful young man. Ask the Lord to work in your heart too and make you useful in His kingdom.

QUESTIONS

- What did the young man do with the rented house?
- How did he get people to come?
- What did he build?
- How did God bless his efforts?

THINK

- Can children be useful in God's kingdom? How?
- How can you be useful to God?

PRAYER

Make me useful in Thy kingdom.

Who Made It?

Thou, even thou, art Lord *alone; thou hast made heaven, the heaven of heavens, with all their host, the earth, and all things that are therein, the seas, and all that is therein, and thou preservest them all; and the host of heaven worshippeth thee.*

—NEHEMIAH 9:6

Sir Isaac Newton was a mathematician and a physicist who lived from 1642–1727. He made important discoveries about light and gravity. He had a friend who was also a great scientist, but he was an atheist. Newton tried to make this man understand that it was God who had created the universe. His friend, however, refused to believe it.

Newton hired someone to make a replica of our solar system in miniature. In the center was a large yellow ball representing the sun, and revolving around this were smaller balls fastened to the ends of rods of varying lengths, representing Mercury, Venus, Earth, Mars, Jupiter, Saturn, in their proper order. (Uranus and Pluto had not yet been discovered.) When he turned the handle, the balls moved in perfect harmony around the sun.

One day, as Newton sat reading in his study, his friend stepped into the room. Immediately he noticed the replica of the planets around the sun, and being a scientist, this friend knew what it represented. When he turned the handle, he exclaimed at the way the planets orbited the sun. Turning to Newton, the man said, "My! What an incredible thing this is! Who made it?"

Without looking up from his book, Newton replied, "Nobody."

The man looked confused. "I don't think you understand what I asked. Who made this thing?"

Looking his friend in the eye, Newton repeated, "Nobody."

The astonished atheist answered heatedly, "You must think I'm a fool! Of course, somebody made this, and he is a genius! I'd like to know who it is!"

Laying his book aside, Newton rose and walked over to his friend. "This small imitation of the solar system amazes you. I cannot convince you that no one made it. Yet, you profess to believe that the great original from which this design is taken has come into being without designer or maker. Now, explain to me how you can draw such a conclusion."

All at once, the man realized his foolishness. Speechless, he left the room. He had a lot of rethinking to do! After much prayer, searching the Scriptures, and speaking with Newton, he came to know that "the Lord, he is the God" (1 Kings 18:39).

QUESTIONS

- Who was Sir Isaac Newton?
- What did he try to explain to his scientist friend?
- What did someone make for him?
- What did Newton's friend ask him when he saw it?
- What was Newton's reply?
- What was his explanation for his strange answer?
- What was the effect on his friend?

THINK

- What would you say to someone if they tried to persuade you there is no God?
- Can everything be explained? Why or why not?

PRAYER

Help me always to believe that Thou art God
and to live like I believe it.

—14—

Timely Words

But these are written, that ye might believe that Jesus is the Christ, the Son of God; and that believing ye might have life through his name.

—JOHN 20:31

In March 1878, a man stepped aboard a streetcar in the city of New York. Before taking his seat, he gave to each passenger a little card on which were printed these words: "Look to Jesus when tempted, when troubled, when dying." Underneath was printed this scripture: "Look unto me, and be ye saved, all the ends of the earth: for I am God, and there is none else" (Isaiah 45:22).

One of the passengers carefully read the card, and then tucked it into his coat pocket. Before he left the streetcar, this man thanked the man who had distributed the cards. "Sir, I was on my way to the ferry, intending to jump from the boat and drown myself. My wife and son both died this past week, and I had no desire to live anymore. However, this card has given me some hope. Do you have anything else for me to read? Do you know a good church for me to attend?"

The man, of course, was more than happy to help this man. Not only did he tell him about a church he could attend, but he also spoke with him about the Lord Jesus Christ, the hope of the world. He gave him a tract to take with him, and promised to visit him the next day. This grieving man began his day without hope or comfort, but God sent him a message of encouragement through a faithful servant. "As I live, saith the Lord God, I have no pleasure in the death of the wicked; but that the wicked turn from his way and live: turn ye, turn ye from your evil ways; for why will ye die, O house of Israel?" (Ezekiel 33:11).

QUESTIONS

- What did the man give to each passenger on the streetcar?
- Can you remember what it said?
- How did it help one man in particular?

THINK

- What do you think might have happened if the man had not handed out the cards? Why?

PRAYER

Teach me always to look to Thee.
Help me to be a light for Thee.

—15—

Wanting to Confess

Then will I teach transgressors thy ways; and sinners shall be converted unto thee.

—PSALM 51:13

Quite some time ago, the wife of an American missionary was sitting on the veranda of her house in Burma one evening. A native boy from the jungle came running through the opening in the hedge. Coming up to her, he asked eagerly, "Does Jesus Christ live here?"

He was a boy about twelve years old. His hair was matted with dirt, and his clothing was ragged and dirty.

"Does Jesus Christ live here?" he asked again, crouching at the lady's feet.

"Why do you want to know that?" asked the lady.

"I want to see Him. I want to confess to Him," answered the boy urgently.

"Why, what have you been doing, that you want to confess?"

"Does He live here?" persisted the boy. "I want to know! I tell lies and I steal; I do everything bad. I am afraid of going to hell. I want to see Jesus Christ, for I heard that He can help poor sinners and save them from hell. Does He live here? Tell me where I can find Him!"

Although the missionary's wife was touched by the boy's earnestness, she felt she had to test him. "But when God forgives those who confess to Him, He wants them to desire a new heart. God calls for those he forgives to sin no more."

"I want to stop sinning!" exclaimed the boy. "But I can't stop! I don't know how to stop. The evil thoughts are in me, and the bad deeds come out of the evil thoughts. What can I do?"

"You cannot see Jesus Christ, my boy," answered the lady kindly, "but my husband and I are here as His servants to speak for Him."

Then she began to tell him about Jesus: His birth, His life, His suffering, His death, His resurrection, His ascension into heaven, and His return on the clouds. She told Him that He died to save guilty sinners who ask for forgiveness. She told him that He gives His Holy Spirit to live in the hearts of sinners, to make them holy and obedient to God. The boy listened with great interest to what the missionary's wife told him about the Lord Jesus Christ.

The boy happily accepted the invitation to come to the mission school. Never had they seen a child so eager to learn. Every day, the boy had a new question about Jesus. Soon he learned how Jesus pardons the sins of His people and gives them grace to make them obedient to God. This young boy found safety and shelter in the Savior of sinners, and this is true happiness.

QUESTIONS

- What did the boy ask? Why?
- How did the missionary's wife test the boy?
- What did she tell him?
- Where did the boy go to learn more about Jesus?

THINK

- Do your sins bother you?
- Are you better than the people in prison or those who do not go to church? Why or why not?
- What does everyone need?

PRAYER

Make me to love the Lord Jesus Christ
who is the Savior of sinners.

The Living Word

These things speak, and exhort, and rebuke with all authority. Let no man despise thee.
—TITUS 2:15

An atheist was speaking to a group of workers at a mill, trying to convince them that the Bible was only a book of fables. At last, one of the workers asked if he could ask a question.

"Ask any question you please," replied the atheist confidently.

The worker stood up and told his own story. "Thirty years ago, sir, I was the curse of this town. No one who had any respect for himself would speak to me. Sometimes I would feel guilty and try to break with some of my bad habits, but in vain. The temperance society[13] tried their best to help me stop drinking, but I failed so often that they gave up on me. Then the police picked me up. I was brought before the judge and sentenced to prison. The guards tried what they could to improve my behavior, but nothing helped. I tried, the temperance society tried, the police tried, and the prison guards tried to improve me, but nothing worked.

"At last, Jesus Himself worked in my heart. He spoke to me some of the sweetest promises of His Word, such as these: 'Come now, and let us reason together, saith the Lord: though your sins be as scarlet, they shall be as white as snow; though they be red like crimson, they shall be as wool' (Isaiah 1:18). 'Fear thou not; for I am with thee: be not dismayed; for I am thy God: I will strengthen thee; yea, I will help thee; yea, I will uphold thee with the right hand of my righteousness' (Isaiah 41:10). 'And he said unto me, My grace is sufficient for thee: for my strength is made perfect in weakness'" (2 Corinthians 12:9).

"These words," continued the mill worker, "melted my heart and made me a new man. I was dead in sin, and the Lord raised me up and made me His child. The question I have for you is this," he concluded, "if the story of Christ is not true and is a fable, as you say, then how can you explain what has produced so blessed and wonderful a change in my poor sinful heart?"

13. The American Temperance Society was founded in Boston in 1826 to try to stop the distressing effects of alcoholism on American families. This group of concerned citizens encouraged people to sign pledges promising not to drink any alcoholic beverages.

The atheist had no answer to give and remained silent.

"Sir," the working man continued, "you may think what you want to, but the gospel is the power of God unto salvation. His Word is the living Word and will accomplish that which pleases Him!"

My dear almighty Lord,
My Conqueror and King!
Thy scepter and Thy sword,
Thy reigning grace I sing:
Thine is the power; behold I sit,
In willing bonds beneath Thy feet.

Now let my soul arise,
And tread the tempter down;
My Captain leads me forth
To conquest and a crown:
A feeble saint shall win the day,
Though death and hell obstruct the way.

Should all the hosts of death,
And powers of hell unknown,
Put their most dreadful forms
Of rage and mischief on,
I shall be safe, for Christ displays
Superior power and guardian grace.[14]

14. Isaac Watts.

QUESTIONS

- What was the atheist trying to tell the workers at the mill?
- Why did one of the workers say he was the "curse of the town"?
- Who tried to improve this man's behavior?
- Who finally changed the man?
- What was one of the verses he quoted?
- What question did he ask the atheist?

THINK

- What would you say to an atheist?

PRAYER

Teach me the saving power of the gospel.

—17—

Tears and a Tract

Therefore I endure all things for the elect's sakes, that they may also obtain the salvation which is in Christ Jesus with eternal glory.

—2 TIMOTHY 2:10

When Richard Knill was a young man, he distributed tracts to men in the army. He would pass out tracts and talk with some of the men. Michael was a soldier who was well liked because of his easygoing, friendly nature. However, he had two faults: he hated religion, and he swore and cursed terribly when he was angry or upset.

Michael walked by one day when Richard Knill was speaking to the men and handing out tracts. Richard, as was his custom, greeted him politely and handed him a tract. Michael, who normally would have politely returned the greeting, instead grabbed the tract angrily. Dangling it in the air, he swore at it, and then said to Mr. Knill, "Are you going to convert me?"

Mr. Knill replied, "Swearing at the tract will not hurt the tract, but it will hurt your soul."

This made Michael very angry. "Make a circle around the preacher," commanded Michael to the other soldiers. "I'm going to give him a piece of my mind."

The men formed a circle around Richard Knill, and Michael swore so terribly that the tears rolled down Mr. Knill's cheeks.

Many years after this painful experience, Mr. Knill went to another city to preach the gospel in the open air. In the midst of the congregation, a tall, gray-headed man listened with great interest and sometimes shed tears. After the service, the man approached Mr. Knill.

"Do you remember the soldier who swore at you because you handed him a tract?" asked the man.

"Yes, sir, I most certainly do," answered Mr. Knill.

"I am that soldier, Mr. Knill. I never forgave myself for that wicked behavior, but I hope it has led me to repentance and that God has forgiven me."

Now Mr. Knill shed tears again, but this time, they were tears of joy. Who would have thought that this man could be saved? By this story, we see that God delights to save sinners, and that no one is too sinful for God to redeem. "Who is a God like unto thee, that pardoneth iniquity, and passeth by the transgression of the remnant of his heritage? He retaineth not his anger for ever, because he delighteth in mercy" (Micah 7:18).

QUESTIONS

- Who was Richard Knill? What did he do?
- Who was Michael? What were his characteristics, both good and bad?
- What was Michael's reaction to Richard's tract?
- Why did Richard cry?
- What did Richard learn when he met Michael years later?
- Why did Richard cry this time?

THINK

- What did you learn from this story?
- Have you ever grieved someone because of your behavior?

PRAYER

Forgive me for the pain I have caused others.
Help me to bring joy to others and to glorify Thee.

—18—

The Good One Penny Did

Now he that ministereth seed to the sower both minister bread for your food, and multiply your seed sown, and increase the fruits of your righteousness.

—2 CORINTHIANS 9:10

Eric was a little boy of about seven years of age. His sister Lydia was putting some things in a small box to send to a missionary working in India.

"Eric," she began, "would you like to put something in this box too?"

Eric had just begun saving up to buy a new toy for himself. So far, he had only one penny.[15] "I haven't got anything except one penny, and I'd rather keep it," answered Eric.

Eric could not stop thinking about the box his sister was planning to send to India, however. He really did want to put something in that box. "But what good is a penny?" wondered Eric. Feeling guilty about his selfishness, Eric went back to his sister and offered her his penny. "The poor people in India need this more than I need my new toy. I want to give them my penny."

Lydia smiled proudly at her little brother. "That's very kind of you, Eric, but the people in India use different money than we do, so your penny wouldn't help them. Why don't you see if you can buy something with your penny and then you can put that in the box?"

"But what should I buy?" asked Eric.

"Maybe you can buy a tract," suggested Lydia. Eric was a child who loved the Lord Jesus. He was used to asking for God's help in everything he did. Therefore, before he went to buy a tract, Eric went to his bedroom, laid the penny on the bed, and knelt down. "Lord," he prayed, "I'm sorry for being selfish about this penny. This is all the money I have, but I really want to give it to Thee now to use in India. I would like to buy a tract with this penny to put in Lydia's box. Please help me find just the right one, and bless it, Lord. Use it to teach someone in India about Thee, for Jesus' sake. Amen."

Then Eric went to the bookstore a few blocks away from his house and bought a

15. A century ago, a penny would have been worth much more than it is today.

tract. Excitedly, he ran home. "Lydia!" he called. "I bought a tract!" He told her that he had asked the Lord to help him choose a tract and to bless it to someone in India. With the faith of a child, he was convinced that God would use it for someone's salvation in a faraway country.

Lydia, who was also a child of the heavenly King, was so touched by Eric's cheerful giving that she wrote about it in the blank page in the back of the tract before she placed it in the box.

At last, the box arrived in India, at the home of the missionary, Mr. Clark. This missionary was trying to learn the language of a tribe which lived some distance away. These people seemed eager to hear the gospel. In fact, one of the chiefs of that tribe was helping Mr. Clark learn their language. This chief came almost every day to Mr. Clark's home to teach him the language, in exchange for food and clothing. The missionary could not help noticing, however, that the chief was more interested in the payment than the work itself. He did not seem to understand the importance of the book Mr. Clark was working on.

On the day that Lydia's box came, the chief was just about to leave for home. "Wait!" called Mr. Clark. "Don't go without taking something with you. This box just came today. Why don't you choose a few things to take home with you?"

So that is how the chief, who could read English very well, came to read the tract that Eric had prayerfully sent to India. The chief read the tract and was touched by the words Lydia had added. He began to read the Bible the missionary had given him. This brought him to Jesus, and he became a child of God. At last, he understood why Mr. Clark worked so diligently on this book. This chief now wanted his whole tribe to learn the precious gospel, and he never rested until God sent them a missionary to live among his people and preach the gospel to them.

Before long, a chapel was built in that village, and many of the natives attended the services and became true Christians. They were earnest followers of Jesus and went into the neighboring villages to tell the people what they had learned about the Savior of sinners. God's blessing accompanied those efforts, and the result was that, within five years from the time Eric's tract was placed in the hands of the chief, several hundred people were brought to the Lord Jesus Christ.

Children, ask the Lord for a new heart, so that you too may belong to Jesus. Ask Him to make you useful in His kingdom. It is a joy to work for the Lord and to honor Him. These are the words of the Savior Himself who says to you, "Come unto me, all ye that labour and are heavy laden, and I will give you rest. Take my yoke upon you, and learn of me; for I am meek and lowly in heart: and ye shall find rest unto your souls. For my yoke is easy, and my burden is light" (Matthew 11:28–30).

QUESTIONS

- What was Lydia doing?
- What did Eric want to use his penny for at first?
- What did Lydia suggest he do with his penny?
- What did Eric do before he bought a tract?
- What did Eric believe God would do with his tract?
- What did Lydia do before she placed the tract in the box?
- How was Mr. Clark learning the tribe's language?
- What did he offer the chief? What did he choose?
- What did the chief finally understand?
- How did God bless Eric's tract?

THINK

- What did you learn from this story?
- What can you do to help mission work?

PRAYER

Bless those who bring Thy Word
all over the world. Give me a willingness
to do what I can to help them.

—19—

Real Christianity

And walk in love, as Christ also hath loved us, and hath given himself for us an offering and a sacrifice to God for a sweetsmelling savour.

—EPHESIANS 5:2

Mr. Parker was a godly man who lived in New York City in the early 1900s. He often spent a part of each Sunday afternoon trying to do some good. He would always pray before venturing out, for he realized that without Jesus' help we can do nothing (John 15:5), but "with God all things are possible" (Matthew 19:26).

The wharves in New York were always filled with noise and activity. People were constantly coming and going. Strong men loaded and unloaded cargo from large ships; exhausted immigrants came off ships looking for a new life in America; weeping friends and relatives said goodbye to people leaving for another country. It was not a safe place, however. Pickpockets, murderers, drunks, and rough men spent much of their time wandering the streets near the wharves. Dishonest men searched out confused, overwhelmed immigrants to trick them into handing over their money by promising them help they did not intend to give. Mr. Parker was not afraid, however. He was eager to assist the poor and sick, but mostly his desire was to bring God's Word to the people whom God placed in his way.

One Sunday afternoon, he met a man named Max who was known in that area for his wicked life. He had already spent time in prison for stealing. Mr. Parker approached him and put his hand on his shoulder. "My friend," he said kindly, "do you know the Lord Jesus Christ?"

Angrily, Max turned and glared at Mr. Parker. "Who do you think you are, talking to me about religion? You Christians are all the same! You think you are better than everybody else is! You love to preach at people, and tell us how awful we are, but what do you actually do for us?"

The wind swirled across the wharves and between the alleys, picking up trash and scattering it. Dark clouds raced across the January sky. It would probably snow that night. Max wore some ragged pants and a thin shirt. He had no coat.

"Why don't you show me your religion by giving me your coat?" challenged Max, a sour grin on his face.

Without hesitation, Mr. Parker took off his coat and threw it around Max's shoulders. Max was too surprised to say anything for a moment. Then, taking the coat off, he held it out to Mr. Parker. "I—I was only joking," he stammered. His voice held no anger now. "I just wanted to see if your religion was real."

Mr. Parker made no move to take the coat back. Max fingered the fine coat. "You really wanted to give this to me?" he asked hesitantly.

"Take it, Max," said Mr. Parker firmly. "You're right. I should have given you my coat before I started preaching to you about God."

"I can see you are a real Christian," replied Max. "What did you want to tell me?"

Mr. Parker smiled a smile that reflected the joy and thanksgiving in his heart. He was cold, but he did not mind. His heart was praising God and, at the same time, asking His help in leading this man to Jesus. "Come with me," urged Mr. Parker, "and I will tell you all about the Lord Jesus Christ, who loves to save sinners."

Mr. Parker took Max home. Over a warm meal, he told his new friend about the Savior. They went to church together where he heard more about the love of God for unworthy sinners. Over time, the Holy Spirit blessed the gospel to Max's heart, and he too began to tell others about his Savior. He could not keep this wonderful news to himself but went back to the wharves and slums of New York, bringing many people the glorious message of love and forgiveness. He never forgot the "real Christianity" Mr. Parker had shown in giving him his own coat, so he rented a small building so he could help those in need. Mr. Parker helped him get donations of clothing and food so that he could offer people something to eat and warm clothes to wear. Max often quoted this verse as he urged people to believe in the Lord Jesus: "This is a faithful saying, and worthy of all acceptation, that Christ Jesus came into the world to save sinners; of whom I am chief" (1 Timothy 1:15).

Children, there have been, and are, many people like Max whom the Lord has saved. You have heard the gospel so many times already. Do not take it for granted! Think seriously about your soul, about eternity, about the Lord Jesus Christ. Remember the promise that Jesus Himself made: "Behold, I stand at the door, and knock: if any man hear my voice, and open the door, I will come in to him, and will sup with him, and he with me" (Revelation 3:20).

QUESTIONS

- Where did Mr. Parker live?
- What did he do every Sunday afternoon?
- Why were the wharves a dangerous place?
- Who was Max?
- What was Max's response to Mr. Parker's question?
- What was Max's challenge to Mr. Parker?
- How did Max know Mr. Parker was a real Christian?
- What else did Mr. Parker do for Max?
- What did Max and Mr. Parker do together?

THINK

- What might have happened if Mr. Parker had not given Max his coat? Why?
- Why is it important to help the poor with food and clothing while also telling them about Jesus?

PRAYER

Make me a real Christian. Fill my heart with selfless love for others, just like Jesus.

—20—

A Faithful Witness

A word fitly spoken is like apples of gold in pictures of silver.

—PROVERBS 25:11

It is told that a salesman visited at a large house and rang the doorbell. After waiting some time, an out-of-breath butler answered the door. Seeing it was a traveling salesman, he remarked impatiently, "Do you know how far I have come just to answer the door, and it is only you?"

"No," answered the salesman.

"Well," panted the butler, "I came from the top floor of the house to answer the door, and now I see it is only you!"

Patiently, the salesman answered, "I'm sorry you had to come so far. But I know of Someone who came down much further than that for you."

The butler looked up in surprise. "Really? Who would that be?"

"The Lord Jesus Christ came all the way down from heaven in order to save sinners," answered the salesman.

The butler was impressed. He had heard vaguely of "religion" but never thought it applied personally to him. The two men formed a friendship, the salesman visiting the butler often on his time off in order to explain more fully the wonderful work of the Savior of sinners.

QUESTIONS

- Why was the butler annoyed?
- What did the salesman reply?
- Why was the butler impressed?

THINK

- What might have happened if the salesman had become angry with the butler?
- Why is it important to be Christlike all the time?

PRAYER

Make me (more and more) like Jesus.

Raymond Jones

And have no fellowship with the unfruitful works of darkness, but rather reprove them.
—EPHESIANS 5:11

Raymond Jones was about twelve years old. He was looking forward to summer vacation. His father had promised to ask farmers in the area if Raymond could spend the summer working on their farm. Raymond was thrilled. He loved animals and agriculture and was eager to learn as much as he could about caring for the animals and crops. One of the farmers Mr. Jones spoke to was Mr. Jenkins, who sold butter, eggs, and milk to the Jones family. Mr. Jenkins said he would be happy to have some help on the farm.

As soon as school was out, Raymond packed his suitcase. Early the following morning, he said good-bye to his mother, and then his father drove him to the Jenkins farm. A quick hug from his father, some last words of farewell, and Raymond was ready to start his summer job.

Once on the farm, Raymond settled into a routine. Each morning and evening, he helped with the chores. He helped make butter and cleaned the milk pails. He worked in the vegetable garden and sometimes helped Mr. Jenkins in the fields. Because Raymond was still young and Mr. Jenkins did not want to work him too hard, Raymond was allowed some free time every afternoon. Raymond enjoyed farm life immensely. There was one thing, however, that bothered him terribly. Mr. Jenkins swore often. Raymond did not like that at all. It made him very uncomfortable. The boy knew it was a sin. What should he do? After a few days, Raymond made a decision.

After the morning chores, he spoke to his boss. "Mr. Jenkins, I'd like to go home, please."

Mr. Jenkins was surprised. "What's wrong? Are you not feeling well? Are you homesick?"

"No, sir," answered Raymond.

"Don't you like it here? I thought you were enjoying yourself."

"I love it here," answered Raymond. He took a deep breath. "But I don't like your swearing, sir. You are taking God's name in vain. I love God, and it hurts me when you abuse His name and use other bad language. I'll have to go home."

Mr. Jenkins was silent. It was clear that the boy was truly hurt by the language he was using. Raymond's words had a great effect on the farmer. He knew how much the boy loved the farm and how much it cost him to give it up. He admired Raymond's courage. He also felt ashamed of himself. After a few moments, Mr. Jenkins spoke. "I'll tell you what, Raymond. You stay here on the farm, and I'll quit swearing."

Raymond's face broke into a happy smile. "Really? That is great! Thanks!"

Raymond stayed for the entire summer vacation, and Mr. Jenkins kept his promise. He did not swear anymore that summer or any time after that. Raymond worked for Mr. Jenkins every summer after that, and the two formed a close bond. They learned much from each other—about animals, crops, God, and His Word. Later, Raymond moved away to go to college, but the two never forgot each other. Mr. Jenkins was always grateful that this young boy had dared to confront him on his sin of swearing. How different their lives would have been if Raymond had kept silent!

QUESTIONS

- Where was Raymond going to spend the summer?
- What did Raymond do on the farm?
- What was the one thing he did not like at the farm?
- What did Raymond ask Mr. Jenkins?
- Why did this request have such an effect on Mr. Jenkins?
- What did he promise Raymond?
- Did he keep his promise?
- What was the result?

THINK

- How do you think both Raymond's and Mr. Jenkins's lives would have been different if Raymond had kept silent?
- Do you and your friends use bad language? If so, what should you do about it?
- What do you do when you hear others use bad language?

PRAYER

Fill me with love for Thee so that
I will treasure Thy holy Name.

The Little Schoolboy's Prayer Meeting

So mightily grew the word of God and prevailed.

—ACTS 19:20

A young boy named Michael lived in one of the villages of Connecticut. During the revival of 1857–1858, Michael was converted to God. He wanted others to know the wonder of belonging to God, so he thought of a way to win his friends' hearts to Christ. He was not satisfied with merely living like a Christian, watching carefully over his words and actions, and patiently bearing his classmates' persecutions and ridicule. He also wanted to find a means for their salvation. Asking God for help and his teacher for permission, he told the children in his class that there would be a prayer meeting in the schoolhouse during the lunch break.

The children attended the prayer meeting. Some were curious; some were merely looking for another opportunity to tease Michael. Who would lead the meeting, they wondered? They didn't think their teacher would be willing, since he did not seem very religious. To their surprise, it was Michael who selected the songs, read a passage of Scripture, and prayed aloud. Simply, lovingly, he tried to explain the gospel to his classmates. Some children listened respectfully; others laughed and jeered, trying to break up the little service by their rude comments.

Michael, however, seemed unmoved by these persecutions and continued the meetings daily. Usually the teacher supervised the children on the playground, but one day he decided to check on the children inside the schoolhouse. What he observed astonished him. He saw how determined Michael was, sincerely desiring to help his classmates. The teacher severely reprimanded those who were present only to disturb the devotions. Now the prayer meetings proceeded more quietly, and the children could pay closer attention. Soon some of them became anxious about their souls and repented of their sins. God, in His grace, saved these penitent children.

Their parents noticed the change and were delighted that their children were now more obedient and quick to ask for forgiveness when they transgressed. Mothers and even fathers found time to join their children at the little lunch hour prayer meetings, and before long, several of these parents were seeking for mercy among the little flock of praying lambs. The ministers in the area, hearing this wonderful news, came to see for themselves and eventually took charge of the services. The result was that about sixty people received salvation. Only eternity will reveal what an impact this little boy had on his community.

Young as he was, he had wrestled with God for fruit on his labor, and the Lord had blessed his simple efforts. How much good young Christians may accomplish when they humbly lean on their Lord for guidance! "For Zion's sake will I not hold my peace, and for Jerusalem's sake I will not rest, until the righteousness thereof go forth as brightness, and the salvation thereof as a lamp that burneth" (Isaiah 62:1).

QUESTIONS

- What did Michael wish for his classmates?
- What did he decide to do?
- How did the children respond?
- Whom did the teacher reprimand? Why?
- What did the parents notice?
- What did the parents begin to do?
- What was the result?

THINK

- What did you learn from this story?
- Do you think it was hard or easy for Michael to lead the prayer meeting? Why?
- Do you love the Lord?
- How do you treat children who love the Lord?

PRAYER

Give me boldness to serve Thee wholeheartedly
and to defend those who love Thee.

—23—

The Minister and the Gypsy Boy

I have set watchmen upon thy walls, O Jerusalem, which shall never hold their peace day nor night: ye that make mention of the Lord, keep not silence.

—ISAIAH 62:6

One day a minister in England was walking near a gypsy[16] camp, talking about the Lord Jesus Christ to anyone who would listen. While buying a basket they had made, the minister heard that there was a sick boy in the camp. "Who is the father of this boy?" asked the minister.

"That man with the red and blue shirt," answered the weaver.

The gray-haired minister made his way over to the father. "I've just heard that your son is ill. May I visit him?"

The father looked suspicious. "Are you going to talk about religion to him?"

"No."

The father raised his eyebrows in surprise. "What then?"

"Only about Jesus," answered the minister.

The boy's father shrugged. "Okay, then, you may visit him. But if you talk about religion, I'll set my dog on you!"

The minister entered the tent. On a mat lay a very sick boy, about ten years old. His eyes were closed, and for a moment the minister wondered if he had already passed away. He picked up the boy's limp hand and felt for a pulse. Yes, there it was, but very faint. Then he leaned forward and repeated this verse in the sick boy's ear: "For God so loved the world, that he gave his only begotten Son, that whosoever believeth in him should not perish, but have everlasting life" (John 3:16). He repeated the verse five times.

It seemed like the boy did not even hear the minister. However, when the minister

16. The term "gypsies" refers to a group of people thought to originate from India. Long ago, they were nomadic, that is, they wandered from place to place in groups. Everywhere they went they were treated with suspicion and even cruelty because of their religious beliefs and practices. They made their way into many countries, including America and Canada.

said it the sixth time, the boy opened his eyes and smiled. In a low whisper, he said, "And I never thanked Him! But nobody ever told me! I want to give Him many thanks!" Then, in utter amazement, he continued softly, "And for me, only a gypsy boy! I thank Him with all my heart!"

The minister's heart overflowed with thanksgiving as he kneeled down to offer a prayer over the poor boy. He saw the boy's lips move again. He leaned down to listen, but heard only, "He sent His only Son!" Then the boy fell into an exhausted sleep.

The minister visited the boy every day and brought him what he could to make him more comfortable. The father remained suspicious but made no objections, since the boy clearly looked forward to the minister's visits and gained strength each day. As the boy learned more about the Savior, it was clear that the Holy Spirit was working in his heart. The boy's desire to thank God for sending His Son to save him from his sins was used by God to save other gypsies as well.

QUESTIONS

- What did the minister ask the father of the sick boy?
- What did he repeat to the boy?
- What was the boy's response?
- What was the result of the minister's visits?

THINK

- What did the minister mean when he told the boy's father he wasn't going to talk about religion but only about Jesus?
- Why do you think the minister recited the same verse over and over?
- What does Jesus mean to you?

PRAYER

Help me never to despise Jesus and His sacrifice.

—24—

Changed by the Gospel

Therefore if any man be in Christ, he is a new creature: old things are passed away; behold, all things are become new.

—2 CORINTHIANS 5:17

A missionary at Ningbo, China, saw a Chinese man at his mission hall whom he had never seen before. After the service was over, he went over to him and greeted him. In the course of the conversation, the missionary said to him, "Sir, is this the first time you heard the gospel preached?"

"Yes, sir," replied the stranger, "but I have seen it preached."

At the missionary's puzzled look, the man went on to explain. "I know a man who used to be the terror of his neighborhood. If you spoke a cross word to him, he would shout at you and keep on cursing you for a long time. He was as dangerous as a wild beast. However, when the religion of Jesus Christ took hold of him, he became entirely changed. He has quit smoking. He is honest. You can trust everything he says. He is kind and gentle. He used to be the worst man in the neighborhood, but now he is the best. Tonight I have heard the gospel preached; but I have seen the gospel preached in watching the life of that man. I want to know more about the religion which can make so good a man out of one who used to be so bad."

What do people notice about you, children? Can they tell that you are a Christian? Does your life set an example that will make others want to know the Lord?

QUESTIONS

- What did the missionary ask the man?
- What was his reply?
- Describe the changes in the opium smoker.
- Why did this Chinese man want to know more about the gospel?

THINK

- Why is it important to live the gospel and not just preach it?
- In what ways can you live the gospel?

PRAYER

Give me a new heart so that I may
live the gospel and glorify Thee.

—25—

George Whitefield and the Trumpeter

So then it is not of him that willeth, nor of him that runneth, but of God that sheweth mercy.

—ROMANS 9:16

George Whitefield was a well-known evangelist in the nineteenth century who often preached outdoors. He made several trips to America, speaking to thousands of people. Some people came to listen because they were curious, some came because they wanted to hear the gospel, but some came to make trouble. One of those people who wanted to make a disturbance was a trumpeter who belonged to an English regiment. Along with hundreds of others, this man, carrying his trumpet, gathered to wait for Whitefield to preach. His intention was to blow his trumpet with all his might in the middle of the sermon so that Whitefield could not continue to preach. He chose a place close to the front. More and more people arrived. Everyone wanted to get as close to the front as possible and people pressed closer together in order to be able to hear well. It became very crowded—so crowded, in fact, that the trumpeter's arms were wedged firmly to his side. He could not raise the trumpet to his lips, nor could he leave. He was kept in his place as securely as if he had been rooted to the spot. Helpless, he could only stand and listen.

The Holy Spirit began to work in the heart of this trumpeter as he listened. He was convicted of his sin, especially the sin of wanting to stop God's Word from reaching sinners' ears. After the service, Mr. Whitefield spoke to him, pointing him to the Lord Jesus Christ. From that time, the trumpeter was changed from an enemy to a child of God.

Have you been changed by the work of the Holy Spirit? Either you hate God and the gospel or you love Him. You are either God's enemy or His child. Search your heart; ask the Holy Spirit to shed His light in your heart and to lead you to the Savior. "Take with you words, and turn to the Lord: say unto him, Take away all iniquity, and receive us graciously: so will we render the calves of our lips" (Hosea 14:2).

QUESTIONS

- Who was George Whitefield?
- What was the trumpeter's intention?
- Why couldn't he do what he intended?
- What did the Holy Spirit teach him?

THINK

- Has the Holy Spirit worked in your heart? What has He taught you?

PRAYER

Shed Thy light in my heart and
lead me to the Lord Jesus.

—26—

The Little Missionary

But exhort one another daily, while it is called To day; lest any of you be hardened through the deceitfulness of sin.

—HEBREWS 3:13

A little boy named Tommy lived in a Christian orphanage in Brooklyn. Later he was adopted into a Christian family in Missouri, but this orphanage always had a special place in his heart, for it was there that he first learned to know God. It was at the orphanage in Brooklyn that God met Tommy in mercy and gave him a love for God and for his neighbor.

Living in Brooklyn, near the orphanage, was an old man named Mr. James who never went to church and wanted nothing to do with religious things. When the children of the orphanage played outside, Mr. James would enjoy talking with them as he walked by.

When Tommy learned that Mr. James did not know the Lord, he felt a deep concern for the man's soul. Therefore, the next time Tommy saw Mr. James, he invited him to come to church with him.

"No, no!" exclaimed the old man, "I haven't gone to church in over twenty years, and I don't want to start now!"

"Oh, please come," pleaded Tommy. "It can't hurt! It will be good for you."

"Not me!" replied Mr. James. "You won't catch me going to church. I know better."

Tears came to Tommy's eyes. He could not help it. He had been asking the Lord to save this man, and now he would not come to church. Tommy loved Mr. James, and wanted so much for him to know the Lord Jesus.

The old man noticed Tommy's tears, and just to please his little friend, he gave in and promised he would go with him to church just once. He was actually quite moved by the boy's tears, for he could not remember anyone having shown such concern for him before.

The church service was not as unpleasant as the old man had thought it would be, so he gave in easily to Tommy's pleadings to come a second time. This time, the Holy Spirit pierced Mr. James's heart. The third time, Mr. James came without having to be persuaded, and the fourth time he came on his own. The Holy Spirit convinced him of sin, of righteousness, and of judgment (John 16:8). He was born again and became a new creature in Christ. Everywhere he went, he now talked about the Savior. He often added, "What would have become of me, had it not been for Tommy's tears and pleadings?"

Tommy was a little missionary, enabled by God's grace to lead this man to Jesus. Is it your greatest desire to serve the Lord and honor Him in all that you do? Do you feel any concern for your own soul as well as the souls of others?

QUESTIONS

- Where did Tommy live?
- Who was Mr. James?
- Why was Tommy concerned about Mr. James?
- What did Tommy ask Mr. James to do?
- Why did Mr. James not want to go to church?
- Why did he agree to go?
- Why did he continue to go to church?

THINK

- How was Tommy a missionary?
- What might have happened had Tommy not continued to ask Mr. James to go to church?
- Why must we be concerned about our own souls?
- Why must we be concerned about the souls of others?

PRAYER

Make it my greatest desire to serve Thee
and to lead others to Thee.

A Minister Who Spoke the Truth

Be strong and of a good courage, fear not, nor be afraid of them: for the Lord thy God, he it is that doth go with thee; he will not fail thee, nor forsake thee.

—DEUTERONOMY 31:6

Many years ago, a well-known minister lived in Paris, France. His name was Jean-Baptiste Massillon. He was born in 1663 in Hyères, a small town in France. Not only did God give this man a gift for preaching, but also He blessed him with courage. Though he remained in the Roman Catholic Church all his life, many people were blessed by his preaching. He preached clearly and honestly so that everyone understood his messages. In 1699, Massillon was asked to preach before King Louis XIV of France in Versailles. Shortly after this, he was appointed the court chaplain to the king. The pastor had never changed or softened his message to please his audiences and it was no different now that he was preaching before the king, for he served the heavenly King above all. Louis XIV once said to Massillon, "I have heard many great orators ... and have been highly pleased with them; but whenever I hear you, I go away displeased with myself, for I see my own character."

Before he died, King Louis XIV gave instructions that he was to be buried in a golden coffin. He stated that at his funeral service he wanted the entire cathedral to be dark, with just one candle lit by his coffin. Even in death, Louis wanted everyone to be impressed by his greatness. In 1715, when Louis XIV died, Massillon was asked to preach the funeral sermon. Everything was arranged just as the king had planned it. The service was held in the beautiful old Cathedral of Notre Dame. The large building was crowded with people. The new king, Louis XV, and all the nobility of France were present. The great congregation was seated and waiting for the minister to appear. The silence of death was there. At last, the Reverend Massillon entered. He walked over to a table on which stood a little golden urn. In the urn was a lock of King Louis XIV's hair. In silence, the minister picked up the little jar and held it in his hands. Moment after moment passed while the minister continued to hold the urn. Slowly, the Reverend Massillon raised the little urn high; his clear, solemn voice was distinctly heard in every part of that great cathedral as he began his funeral sermon with these startling words, "Only God is great!"

The greatness of the dead king had passed away like a dream. The courageous pastor wanted to tell the people that the greatness of man is nothing compared to the almighty, eternal God of heaven and earth. Earthly kings will fade and die, but God's greatness will never pass away; God will never die.

You will not live forever either, children. One day you must appear before the great King of Kings and He will judge you to determine your eternal future. Are you ready for this important day? Do you serve God or are you rebelling against Him? Ask the Holy Spirit to give you a new heart that serves Him only. That is the only way to be safe and to be truly happy.

QUESTIONS

- Who was Jean-Baptiste Massillon?
- Before whom was he asked to preach?
- Did he soften his message? Why not?
- Why was the king displeased?
- What were King Louis XIV's instructions for his funeral? Why?
- What did Massillon pick up and hold in his hands?
- What did he finally say? Why?

THINK

- What do you imagine the people's reactions were?
- What is most important in this life?
- What is most important to you? Why?

PRAYER

Help me to understand what is most important.

—28—

A Teacher's Tear

A soft answer turneth away wrath: but grievous words stir up anger.

—PROVERBS 15:1

At the end of one of his Sunday school classes, Mr. Douglas asked a girl named Sarah to remain behind. Sarah had not been paying attention but had whispered and giggled during class. "Sarah, I have a question for you," said Mr. Douglas quietly. He paused and she looked up at him, her eyes flashing with anger. He asked, "What would happen to your soul if you were to die tonight?"

Sarah was annoyed at the startling question. She looked away. What right had he to ask her this? He just wanted to make her feel bad. Well, it was not going to work! She looked up at him again, ready to give an angry reply, but fell silent when she looked at his kind, gentle face. A large tear rolled down Mr. Douglas's cheek. In a moment, her anger vanished. He was not her enemy—he was her friend! That tear, coming from a heart filled with loving concern, pierced her heart. Soon Sarah was crying too—tears of shame.

Sarah always thought fondly of that turning point in her life. It was not so much the question, but the love of God, evident in Mr. Douglas's tear, that stopped her. She thanked the Lord for His goodness in showing her what really lived in her heart, but also what lives in God's heart. She would spend an eternity thanking the Lord Jesus Christ for waking her up from her sleep of death, for saving her from her sins, and for placing her on the pathway to life eternal.

QUESTIONS

- Why did Mr. Douglas ask Sarah to remain after class?
- What did he ask her?
- Why was Sarah angry?
- What took away Sarah's anger? Why?
- What was the result?

THINK

- What might have happened, had the teacher angrily scolded Sarah? Why do you think so?
- Can we cause God grief even when we are outwardly well-behaved? How?

PRAYER

Help me to be obedient and respectful
to my parents and teachers.

—29—

Little Brother's Warning

And be ye kind one to another, tenderhearted, forgiving one another, even as God for Christ's sake hath forgiven you.

—EPHESIANS 4:32

Three children were learning their verse after breakfast one morning. Their mother recited it with them until they knew it perfectly. After cleaning up the breakfast dishes, the children were going outside to play but Nancy and Frank, the two elder children, began to quarrel. Nancy wanted to play with the big ball, but Frank wanted it too.

"You are mean!" shouted Nancy.

"You're selfish!" answered Frank.

"I'll tell Daddy what a mean boy you are," said Nancy.

"And I'll tell Mommy I wish she would sell you. I don't want you for my sister," responded Frank.

"I don't love you one bit," said Nancy.

"Who cares?" Frank taunted.

The children carried on, from bad to worse, saying all sorts of unkind, unpleasant things to each other. While this was going on, their little brother, Benny, came up behind them. As he listened to the angry words, he looked very surprised and his big blue eyes opened wider and wider. Benny was barely two years old, but he could see that Nancy and Frank were not being good.

When the two children began pulling at the ball, Benny said in his baby language, "Little children, love one another."

They had just been learning the verse. Nancy and Frank stopped what they were doing and looked at each other and blushed.

"Here, Frank," said Nancy, "you can have it. I'll play with something else."

"Why don't we play together?" suggested Frank. "I'm sorry I was mean to you."

"I'm sorry too," Nancy confessed.

Then they went outside together to play.

QUESTIONS

- What were Frank and Nancy doing?
- What did Benny say?
- How did Frank and Nancy respond?

THINK

- Have you ever quarreled with your siblings?
- Why is it hard to be kind and loving to our siblings?
- What can we do to change that?

PRAYER

Forgive me for my sins against my siblings.
Give me a heart that is kind, patient, and loving.

—30—

Blessing for Food

[Jesus] looked up to heaven, and blessed, and brake the loaves.

—MARK 6:41

A sailor came home from a voyage. He was glad to be home again. It had been so long since he had seen his family! When he arrived at his house, it was late in the evening and the children were already asleep. The sailor's wife greeted him joyfully and quickly prepared a plate of food for him. To her dismay, the wife noticed that he sat down and began to eat without thanking his heavenly Father who had so kindly provided his daily bread.

The next morning, his excited children greeted him. Finally, they sat down to eat breakfast. Again, the sailor began to eat without giving thanks. His eldest child, a four-year-old girl, looked at him in astonishment. After a moment, she asked, "Daddy, don't you ask a blessing on your food?"

The sailor was especially fond of his only daughter, and her gentle rebuke pierced his heart. He sat stunned, thinking about her question. The girl turned to her mother as if pleading for support, and said, "We pray for our meals now, don't we, Mommy?"

The man's eyes were riveted on his daughter's pain-filled face, and it suddenly struck him that he had never taught her to pray. He had never set an example for his children by praying with his family when he was at home, though he himself had been taught to do so. He laid down his knife and fork, and said, "Would you like to ask the blessing this morning, Nancy?"

The child, seeing her father waiting for her to begin, put her hands together, lifted her eyes to heaven, and uttered the most trusting prayer the sailor had ever heard. Nancy's searching question and her simple prayer was the beginning of the sailor's conversion. God used this little girl to convict the sailor of his godless ways. His thanklessness became his guilt. He confessed his sin and found forgiveness with the Lord Jesus Christ.

QUESTIONS

- Why was the sailor's wife dismayed?
- What did the sailor's daughter ask him?
- What was his response?
- How did her question and prayer affect the sailor?

THINK

- Why is it important to pray before meals?
- Why is it important to pray every day?
- Is prayer important to you? How?

PRAYER

Teach me to pray.